Following The LAMB

Befriending Jesus and Sharing Him

PETE DARNELL

Following the Lamb: Befriending Jesus and Sharing Him

By Pete Darnell

Printed in the United States of America

ISBN: 978-1-63315-532-9

Design by AdvanceGraphics.us

Contents

Addendums

Dedicated
to our children
Jeff, Josh, & Jenny
who follow the Lamb
(our greatest joy)

Introduction

Like many other Christians, I was enthusiastic for Christ following my conversion at age twelve. I don't remember now all the particulars, but somewhere along the way I replaced that personal friendship I had with Christ with the satisfaction of being in a good church and the right movement. I'm not sure when and where it happened. It was a process over time encouraged by some success and applause.

I was the pastor of a growing church when I admitted that there was something terribly wrong. Some wondered why I would leave the ministry I loved, move to a farm house on a dirt road in rural Tennessee, and find a regular job. The reason is that I had only a "third person" relationship with the Lord. I was hungry for something better than that.

Through John 15:4 I discovered that *Jesus* is more than a doctrine. He is available to each in His family as a friend! This is what I had been missing! I knew I was saved by grace through faith alone, and I knew how to separate from some sins, but I didn't know what it was to walk with Christ every day. I remember leading someone to Christ and being envious of their pure, simple joy and thinking "That probably won't last long!"

It still amazes me that friendship with Christ is so simple. He *is* the love-gift from the Father to every believer in His Church. A gift is not a complicated thing. Jesus is the satisfaction of our thirst for reality. He is the "what" of our quest. But what is the "how?" Hopefully this book will answer that question.

I have known a few people who are driven by this passion. They are consumed by Christ and the Word. The written Word and the personal Word are one. The written Word is the catalyst for friendship with Jesus. When we see truth in the Word we are looking directly into the face of Jesus Christ who is "the truth" (John 14:6). I talk with all my friends when I see them, and it's easy to talk with my best friend as I see Him in the Word.

Synopsis of Personal Holiness

The Bible speaks of the Christian life in many ways. There are numerous examples, metaphors, and allegories. Having pastored for almost fifty years, the following five statements is a distilled synopsis of how I view the dynamics of the Christian life.

- Friendship with Christ is the cause and effect of real life.
- The Holy Spirit is the agent for this life.
- The Word is the catalyst.
- Meditation in the Word is the method.
- Yielding my spirit to the God of the Word is the continuing first step.

This book will attempt to identify these moving parts of the spiritual life we have been given, qualify our responsibilities, and establish a plan for us and for those we are to disciple. It is an attempt to put into words our occupation with Christ, which is discipleship 101.

Part One

Being a Disciple

Before Jesus ascended into heaven after His resurrection, He introduced the new ministry the Holy Spirit was to have in the new church period (John 14-16). One of the things He is to be doing now is to glorify Christ (John 16:14). The Holy Spirit primarily does this through the Word. Since we were saved, we believers have had a fascination with Jesus, that is, unless sin has broken that friendship.

Part One may help you identify what makes the Christian life tick. Its goal is for you to learn how to establish and maintain friendship with Jesus as a lifestyle.

CHAPTER 1

Friendship with Christ

Need

Daily, personal friendship with Christ is the most important need in the Christian's life. The first and greatest commandment is for us to love the Lord totally (Matt. 22.37). The greatest sin then is for us to reject His offer of friendship (John 15:15) and love anyone or any thing more. If, as I suggest, this friendship with Him is the most important factor in our life, surely there can be no success in any area without it. This, however, is not true for the unbeliever. Nothing is more important for the unsaved than his eternal salvation. If you have never accepted Christ's sacrifice on the cross for your sins, please consider John 3:16, repent of your sins, and ask Jesus to save you. He will!

All of us Christians some of the time and many of us much of the time demonstrate that our flesh can exhibit the "works of the flesh" (Gal. 5: 9-21). The Holy Spirit convicts us, and we initially feel terrible, but eventually become numb to conscience and His voice. Attitudes set in our character from our youth or added since fall victim to Satan's temptations and our fallen nature responds exactly like the unsaved around us. None of us want that to happen, but it does consistently when the Holy Spirit is busy convicting and chastening us for our sin instead of His preferred tasks of subjecting the flesh (Rom. 8:13), teaching us (John 14:13), and magnifying the Lord to us (John 16:13-14).

Definition

Friendship with Christ is the door to communion with the Father (1 John 1:3, Matt. 11:27). It is synonymous with abiding in Christ (John 15:4), being "filled with the Spirit" (Eph. 5:18), walking in the Spirit (Gal. 5:16), and the believer's present "rest" (Heb. 4:9). These passages reveal only one concept viewed from different vantage points. God designed man for communion with Himself. Augustine put it this way: "Thou madest us for Thyself, and our heart is restless, until it repose in Thee."[1] All the wicked of the world are without this peace (Isa. 57:20-21). Though we who are saved can have this rest we often do not because we do not live closely with Christ.

Source

The qualification or prerequisite for being a disciple is allowing Christ to be our true source.

Luke 14:25-33 reminds us of the cost of discipleship: love Jesus more than family, accept suffering, and follow Christ. Then, after the allegories of a builder foolishly under-estimating the cost of building and a general not having enough soldiers to win the battle, Jesus said, "so likewise, whosoever he be of you that forsaketh not all that he hath, he cannot be my disciple." Or, put another way, if we allow any other spring to satisfy us more than this fountain, we may be saved but do not qualify as a disciple. There are many evil and neutral substitutes available to us. The world is full of alternatives to Christ. For the believer there are other tangents, which may not be sin, but, if allowed to preempt Christ, become a challenge to His supremacy.

In Luke 14, the two things we are likely to put ahead of Jesus are our family (v. 26) and the things we have (v. 33). 1 John 2:16 reminds us that the sins of the body, covetousness, and selfish ambition are substitutes for loving the Lord. "And the cares of this world, and the deceitfulness of riches, and the lusts of other things" are thorns that render the Word ineffective (Mk. 4:19).

An objective analysis of our own emptiness and the challenges of discipleship should make us aware of our need of help and make Christ's offer more desirable.

So, what is this friendship with Jesus? It is enjoying the reality of life as God defines it in communion with Jesus and sourced only in Him.

Distinction

There is a difference between outward Christianity and its inward reality.

There is nothing more important than friendship with Jesus. If the believer is "complete in Him" alone (Col. 2:10), certainly all the other factors of the Christian life must find their relevance in Christ alone. He is more important than prayer for the things we need, more urgent than Bible study, more essential than obeying God, more influential than soul winning, more beneficial than preaching or listening to the Word preached, more satisfying than family, more significant than building a church, and more effective than the community of believers. All these are the results of the right relationship with Christ. It is very possible to have our lives full of religious things and suddenly realize that we are empty. Burnout among God's people is becoming epidemic partly because we have repositioned our "first love" (Rev. 2:4). As individuals and churches we must not allow any goal or purpose to get more attention than our Lord.

The reason that the majority of professing Christians will miss the rapture is because most of the churches have assumed Christ in His absence. We have replaced the Head of the Church with Biblical goals and objectives. He doesn't play second fiddle!

We must have a desire for the Lord Himself more than for the things of the Lord. Every new believer has a hunger for the Lord that often diminishes as he or she refocuses on church things or the things of the world. In grace God chastens us (Heb. 12:4-12). When He gets our attention, we confess (1 John 1:9), and that desire for the Lord is renewed. Friendship with the Lord is the result of a diligent search (Jer. 29:13, Luke 11:9-10). Though the Lord chooses to be anonymous, and though He is not found parading in public, the diligent heart is the object of His interest. In fact, while on the road of discovering Him, it is a happy moment to learn that He has been seeking us (John 4.23)!

There is a distinction between pursuing God and the things of God.

Reading the Bible

How does a mortal have fellowship with God? Let's get right to the heart of the matter. The Bible is the most important book ever written. All believers know the Bible is significant because it reflects its author, God. We were "born again . . . through the living and abiding word of God" (1 Pet.1:23, ESV). We remember the knife of conviction for our sin and the healing gospel all from the Word. Now that we believe, the Book is important to us because it changes those who look at the Lord in it (2 Cor. 3:18). It is more beneficial than other books because the Bible is the only writing that is inerrantly inspired by God (2 Tim. 3:16).

There are three methods of reading the Bible. Each has a worthy objective, and in time every believer should employ each of them to some degree. One can adapt these modes to his needs.

The first method is to read larger portions to gain familiarity with the themes of the Bible and to get an overview of its teaching. Numerous reading schedules are available online or at any Christian bookstore. The New Testament is the best place to start. It will be helpful to have the benefit of a study Bible. This type of reading provides balance and an opportunity to enjoy the broad scope of this wonderful Book.

The second mode is to read less than the above method in order to spend more time in study of a passage. Instead of reading several chapters, read a paragraph or less. Take advantage of a commentary on that particular book of the Bible. There are good single volume commentaries you may purchase, and your pastor may be willing to loan you some books from his library. It is important that the books you buy or borrow adhere to the traditional, conservative view of interpretation. Unfortunately there is misleading material written about the Bible by liberals and some evangelicals who have a different agenda.

The third way to read the Bible is to read it responsively to interact with God. Although the former two methods need little explanation, this type of reading needs more emphasis because it is the most important of the three methods for every Christian. Reading to cultivate friendship with God is critical, because God wants that intimacy with you (1 John 1:1-7, John 14:21-23, 15:4-11, Ps. 42:1-5).

To those who have labored beyond their strength and to those who are heavy laden beyond their ability, the invitation of Jesus to "come unto me . . . and I will give you rest" (Matt.11:28-30) is a most welcomed hope for the weary soul. He befriends the needy!

It is an awesome thought that God has created you to entertain His very presence! This is a valuable reason to read this wonderful book. In practical terms, the way to read the Bible responsively is to integrate reading and prayer.

Praying the Bible

The Bible is the catalyst for friendship with the Lord. We are not talking about earning a Bible degree. Just read it slowly and respond to the Lord regarding the thought you've just read. If you don't understand the verse or paragraph, skip over it to something you can understand. Maybe you can ask someone about what you don't understand or study it out for yourself later, but the important thing here is to not get bogged down with study. The Word is full of wonderful, powerful truths that are laying right out on top of the page! You don't need to be a scholar or even a smart person to gather the ripe fruit that is easily picked! The Bible was not written primarily for preachers to preach, but for believers to have and to hold close in order to know their God.

Simply read a phrase with your mind, yield your spirit to it, and respond to the Lord, who is closer than the Bible you are reading! Enjoy His presence through the Word for a while, and take a verse or a phrase with you for the day to extend that connection.

For example, open your Bible to Psalm 23:1. Read the first phrase. "The Lord is my shepherd." Stop reading. Now talk to God about what He said to you. You may respond to Him with praise for who He is, with thanks for leading you, with confession of the sin of not following Him, or with a prayer for someone you know that needs His leadership right now. Read the second phrase of that verse. "I shall not want." Stop reading. As if in conversation with the Author over the phone, respond to what He just said to you. "I shall not want" means that while following this Shepherd He will provide what I need. You may want to thank Him for His past provisions, for the promise of good things in the future, or for the love that prompted Him to care for you.

The Bible contains all God wants to say to you now. Prayer is what you say to God. Robert Murray McCheyne was a nineteenth century Presbyterian pastor in Scotland who enjoyed God and is one of my heroes. He wrote, "Turn the Bible into prayer. Thus, if you were reading the first Psalm, spread the Bible on the chair before you, and kneel, and pray, 'Oh Lord, give me the blessedness of the man . . . let me not stand in the counsel of the ungodly.' This is the best way of knowing the meaning of the Bible, and of learning to pray."[2]

Areas of Prayer

Many Christians agree that there are five areas of prayer. Worship is praising God for who He is. Thanksgiving is recognizing His many blessings. Confession is admitting our sins. Petition is asking God for what we need. Intercession is praying for someone else. To "turn the Bible into prayer" read a phrase or verse then pray to God in response to what the verse says. For example, if you read something that reminds you of a sin, confess that sin immediately. If the verse makes you think of something you need, ask God for it. If the Spirit draws your attention to another person, spend a short time praying for their needs. If your reading tells you something about God, repeat that back to Him as worship. When you see something God has done for you, give Him thanks. Who God is and what He has done often go together. So worship and thanksgiving are closely related as in Revelation 1:5-6.

> Unto him that loved us, and washed us from our sins in his own blood, And hath made us kings ("a kingdom"- NAS) and priests unto God and his Father; to him be glory and dominion for ever and ever. Amen.

The same thing is in Revelation 4:11. "Thou art worthy, O Lord, to receive glory and honor and power: for thou hast created all things, and for thy pleasure they are and were created."

If you follow this method of reading, your heart will sense the Lord's presence in His Word and you can worship freely. The important thing to remember is that when you read the Bible, God is there in His Word actually communicating with you. Your spirit must be yielded to whatever He says. No one comes into His presence who is not on their knees inwardly. Any other attitude is the result of sinful pride. Although chapters may be read with the mind, God will not be found. However, He is near the humble (Ps. 51:17). The first step to obeying the Scriptures is to spiritually bow before the God of the Word as you read.

For many years my devotional time with the Lord was divided between reading the Bible and praying. I struggled with a wandering mind, with the Bible seeming impersonal, and with being unaware of God's comfort, or the Lord's presence. My spirit was not broken. My sinful nature still fights against my desire to commune with God, but this simple plan has helped me greatly.

George Muller was a prayer warrior! For the needs of his several orphanages in nineteenth century England, he told no one but God, Who faithfully answered. It was Muller's practice for some years to read his Bible and then to pray. After learning to integrate reading and praying, he wrote in 1841:

> After a few minutes my soul had been led to confession, or thanksgiving, or intercession, or supplication, yet it turned almost immediately to prayer. When thus I have been for a while making confession, or intercession, or supplication, or having given thanks. I go to the next words of the verse, turning all as I go into prayer for myself or others, as the Word may lead to it, but still continually keeping before me that food for my own soul as the object of my meditation.[3] (Please see Addendum 1)

The most important element for the believer is daily friendship with Christ through the Word.

God has promised that the Spirit will help guide you (John 16:13). Throughout the day as you think about what you have read, you will grow like a fruit tree planted by a river (Ps. 1:2-3). With God's help (Heb. 13:5-6) you can do this!

---

[1]St. Augustine, *Confessions of Saint Augustine,* 5.

[2]Bonar, Andrew, *Memoirs of McCheyne,* pp. xix-xx of the Biographical Introduction by S. Maxwell Coder.

[3]Steer, Roger, *George Muller Delighted in God!,* pp. 103-104.

CHAPTER 2

Beginning of Friendship

A Broken, Yielded Spirit

The first requirement of man approaching God is contrition (Ps. 51:17, Isa. 57:15, 61:1). Pride is the primary reason many will not repent of their sins to be saved. This absence of brokenness renders even an otherwise Biblical life or ministry useless. One can be full of religion yet empty of God at the same time. In many cases, we are filling our churches with empty people. The first cause of holiness from the human perspective is a spirit that is submissive and yielded to God.

The Lord is nigh unto them that are of a broken heart; and saveth such as be of a contrite spirit (Ps. 34:18).

Definition

If a yielded spirit is so important, what is it? There are three key words in Romans 6: "know, reckon, yield." These provide the outline of our responsibilities to follow Christ. "The practical, daily, and even momentary use of each of these three key words will give us the secret of perpetual holiness."[1] The standard Greek dictionary written by Joseph Thayer defines "yield" with "to place beside or near; to set at hand; to present; to proffer, to provide."[2] Charles Hodge suggests the word means "to place by, to present (as an offering); to give up to the power or service of."[3] W. E. Vine adds "to put a thing at the disposal of another, and so voluntarily to present."[4] In Luke 2:22 this word is used. When Jesus was eight days old He was brought to the temple "to present him to the Lord." Romans 12:1 translates this word the same way by requiring all believers to "present your bodies a living sacrifice." Paul again uses "yield" to describe the church being presented to the Father (2 Cor. 4:14). As a child is given up to the priest for dedication, and as believers will be presented to the Father, the word "yield" means "to give up" as in a presentation.

It is not enough to separate from sin and confess it when we are guilty. We must be proactively Godward. There is no such thing as a neutral zone for the mediocre believer. In Rev. 3.16 to be "lukewarm" is a position that is rejected by the Lord. At every moment we are either walking in the Spirit or fulfilling the lust of the flesh (Gal. 5.16).

If you desire more friendship with Christ, you might pray this prayer with me.

> *Lord, thank you for saving me and allowing me to be your child. In spite of my failures and my many excuses, the Spirit is pointing to you as the only object of worship and the only source of life. Forgive me for assuming you and thereby ignoring you. I don't understand even what I know about you from the Bible, but I do desire to please you. I do yield my spirit to what I see of you in the Word. Help me to see more and to worship you, and help me to live by your strength in such a way that I can stand before you one day with joy and not shame. Amen.*

Distinction

We would all agree that our attitude toward the Lord should always be one of yieldedness. To help us see more clearly what this is, it might be helpful to also understand what it is not. Brokenness begins in the human spirit before it affects the soul. I would distinguish the NT usage of "spirit" and "soul" most of the time. At 1 Thessalonians 5:23 the Old Scofield Study Bible has a most helpful note. In describing the human make-up Dr. Scofield writes that with the body we are world-conscious, with the soul we are self-conscious, and with the spirit we are God-conscious.[5] "Spirit" is "the power of perceiving and grasping divine and eternal things, and upon which the Spirit of God exerts its influence."[6] Martin Luther wrote that the "spirit is the house where faith and God's word are at home."[7] With our spirit we understand the things of God (1 Cor. 2:12-14), we worship (John 4:24), and we know God (Rom. 8:16).

Aristotle described the Greek concept that ones "soul" includes his mind, will, and emotions. I know that some do not distinguish "soul" and "spirit," but certainly they would agree with the functions suggested by each whether or not they would accept the semantics. The important thing to remember is that spiritual life does not reside in one's mind. Intelligence is not a discernible factor in following the Lord. Willpower varies among temperaments and cannot he depended upon (John 1:13). And certainly emotions are a poor barometer to follow. The Spirit desires to control our spirit and reveal Himself through our soul: in mind (1 Cor. 2:16), in will (Phil. 2:13), and in emotions (Gal. 5:22). Christianity is spiritual rather than soulish. To be mentally superior, have a strong will, or be emotionally charged is not an advantage, and can become a distraction. Though God gives each of us special abilities in many areas, the emphasis of Scripture is that we give ourselves over to His control and power. In the final analysis, godliness is mostly God! We make a big mistake in looking within ourselves to discover qualities that are sufficient for the task of pleasing God. He makes impossible demands that can only be realized by divine power.

Everyone yields their spirit to something. Oswald Chambers wrote of the options.

> There is no powering the human soul of itself to break the bondage of a disposition formed by yielding. Yield for one second to anything in the nature of lust . . . and though you may hate yourself for having yielded, you are a bond slave to that thing. There is no release in human power at all but only in the Redemption. You must yield yourself in utter humiliation to the only One Who can break the dominating power viz., the Lord Jesus Christ.[8]

Romans 6 presents two masters or powers (v. 18). Man is not considered to be a third power. His only function here is to yield to God or Satan. In the big picture, God and Satan are in titanic combat. Man's only significance is as he aligns himself with either force. Everyone aligns themselves with either the Lord or Satan as they yield their spirit. The activities of one's soul (thinking, choosing, feeling) reflect the direction of the spirit. The most important thing for the believer is yielding his spirit to the God of the Word every moment so that the Spirit can direct his thinking, choosing, and feeling. Otherwise our sinful flesh is directing us. We cannot but obey the direction of our spirit. Prayer changes us because it allows God to affect our spirit. Rules are ineffective to change one's character because they only affect one's soul and/or body temporarily.

It is a great relief to me to know that the Lord provides all the power for what He expects of me. Many Christians suffer great discouragement from their inability to please God. Some have sincerely tried to obey the Lord with their own strength only to fail consistently. In time they quit trying and sit back with the multitude of could-have-been disciples who have honestly tried and discovered the task to be beyond them. This albatross can be dropped as we realize that the work of God is done by the power of God through yielded insignificants like you and me.

The Bible presents Christ as the head of the Church and the individual for leadership and as the center for daily activities. The relationship that makes both happen is friendship with Christ.

---

[1]W. H. Griffith Thomas, *St. Paul's Epistle to the Romans,* p. 173

[2]Joseph Henry Thayer, *Thayer's Greek-English Lexicon*, p.489

[3]Charles Hodge, *Commentary on the Epistle to the Romans,* p. 205

[4]W. E. Vine, *Epistle to the Romans*, p. 92

[5]*Holy Bible,* Scofield Reference Edition, p. 1270

[6]Thayer, *Thayer's Greek-English Lexicon,* p. 520

[7]quoted by Thayer, ibid. p. 520

[8]Oswald Chambers, *My Utmost for His Highest,* p. 74

CHAPTER 3

Relation of the Word to Friendship

What we do with the Bible and genuine friendship with the Lord are related and that relationship is cause/effect. Jesus said to a group of Jews who had moments earlier "believed on Him" and who apparently wanted to join his band of followers, "If ye continue in my word, then are ye my disciples indeed" (John 8:31).

Those who receive Christ as their Savior are highly motivated initially to become a personal follower of Jesus. McCheyne said, "An awakened soul feels that his chief happiness is in coming before God."[1] Having been forgiven much, the new convert is excited about serving Him. In time, however, many believers lose that satisfying focus and are allured by the siren call of the world. This happens because they have not maintained that bond with the Lord in the Word. When a believer chooses the ways of the world, symptoms begin to show in several areas. But there is one common thread; they have failed to "continue in my word."

I have had the opportunity of personally working closely with chemically dependent men in our city for many years. I have learned that every believer who has established fellowship with Christ through the Word has more than enough strength to overcome the strongest dependency, to endure the most horrid suffering, and to move beyond the direst personal loss. As long as one maintains that attachment to Christ victory continues. But, when one does not "continue in my word," the power of addiction returns.

Everyone is addicted to his sin nature. We cannot keep from sinning by trying harder. As we fail, usually we compensate by restructuring the seriousness of our sin. Adultery, we conclude, is bad, but indifference to the lost souls around us is not so bad. This is exactly how chemically addicted people think.

The first two paragraphs of Romans 6 tell us that addiction to any and every sin was conquered by Jesus on the cross. Romans 8 relates Jesus' success to ours. The miracle of daily victory over sin is directly related to the Word. "Greater is he that is in you than he that is in the world" (1 John 4:4) is the truth!

Psalm 119

Psalm 119 teaches us three things that relate to our subject: the exalted place God has given His Word, the Word's central function to stimulate spirit and life, and man's proper response to God's communication. This Psalm is an acrostic. Each of the eight verses in a section begins with the same Hebrew letter. Scroggie suggests that "It is reasonable to suppose that the acrostic device was designed to assist the memory."[2] We taught our children:

- A—"All we like sheep have gone astray."
- B—"But He was wounded for our transgressions."
- C—"Children obey your parents in the Lord."
- D—"Do all things without murmuring or disputing."
- E—"Even a child is known by his doings," and so on.

But, the Jewish children had eight verses for each letter of their alphabet! All 176 verses but three have a reference to the Word using at least eight synonyms. This Psalm states the importance of the Word in every area of life.

What do I do with the Word each day? Psalm 119 tells us the importance of the Bible and how the writer responds to it. "O how love I thy law! it is my meditation all the day" (v. 97). To him the heart is greatly involved with the Word. It is the believer's only true source book for defining reality and guidance. But to many it has yet to become "the joy and rejoicing of mine heart" (Jer. 15:16).

Word as Catalyst

Three areas of the Word's impact on our heart can be easily noted from Psalm 119, and you could probably add more. First, verses 2 and 10 emphasize that we seek Him with our "whole heart." Though God is obvious through creation (Rom. 1), He is hypothetical to the unbeliever and remains anonymous to the believer who does not "seek him with the whole heart." When our heart is not yielded to the Word, the Lord seems distant. We know He is near, but He is easy to forget. We hear about Him from others, but we don't hear Him ourselves. "Ye shall seek me and find me, when ye shall search for me with all your heart" (Jer. 29:13). The Word is the impetus for this pursuit. The Bible displays God. What we do with His Word we do with Him.

We seek Him with our entire heart via the Word. And it is there that we learn how to obey Him with our whole heart as per verses 34 and 69. Certainly God has the right to require unmitigated allegiance of His people. The present multicultural fog in our nation would define God generically along with other gods. But Jehovah is uniquely defined by the Scriptures, which identify His people by obedience. He has many children living in disobedience, and to that degree they are undistinguished from unbelievers. But the Holy Spirit indwelling every saint would lead us into fellowship, truth, and obedience (John 15:26-16:14). No one follows Christ who is not submitted to the Word. We follow the God of the Word, not contemporary redefinitions for political or social purposes. The Word exhibits God, and our first response must be submission. Scroggie notes, "Whole heartedness for God is the secret of the blessed life."[3] If you are hungry for God, the Word displays Him, and the only ingredient you must bring is a yielded, broken spirit. He will supply everything else.

Second, the Word can "enlarge my heart" (v. 32).

I will run the way of thy commandments, (as) you enlarge my heart (or set my heart free).

Not many believers "run" to God. Most of us walk at best. And many of us run from His commandments for us! The important part of this verse for us is that it is He that enlarges our capacity to obey and pursue Him. God engineers and empowers our maturity according to our association with His Word.

Most believers are discouraged, assuming they could never be what God wants them to be. God's expectations *are* beyond our capabilities. But what we forget is that it is God who enlarges our heart to run successfully. It has been written of Robert Murray McCheyne, "The real secret of his soul's prosperity lay in the daily enlargement of his own heart in fellowship with God."[4] If God really does provide the strength needed, why can't you be what God wants you to be? The real reason is that we don't believe God! We are "unbelieving believers!" It is the Word that enlarges our heart for friendship with God.

Third, the Word is the direction for a Godward heart. "Incline my heart unto thy testimonies" (v. 36). It is the route we go; the course we follow. It is to His "testimonies" that we are to come. We preachers are to "preach the word" (2 Tim. 4:2). It's the Word that people need, not our sermons about the Word. Today there are many substitutes being literally sold to the church. Christian bookstores are full of "how to" manuals for the searching soul. One might get the impression that advice of spiritual gurus is necessary for a Godward heart. "It is not from sitting under any particular ministry that you are to get nourishment, but from being vitally united to Christ."[5] Many Christians read far more extra curricular books than the Bible itself. Even the sacred desk is not exempt from preachers of fortune selling themselves and their words. "I see a man cannot be a faithful minister, until he preaches Christ for Christ's sake—until he gives up striving to attract people to himself, and seeks only to attract them to Christ."[6] Don't forget; only the Bible is inspired of God. And only the Holy Spirit within you can teach you spiritual truth (1 Cor. 2:12-13). Happy is the church whose pastor knows the difference between "oversight" and "being lords over God's heritage" (1 Pet. 5:2-3).

Sacred Cows

If one used the Bible alone for his authority, certainly he would conclude that the Word is the best source to know and experience God. Unfortunately in our society there are many alternatives. For some it's just not necessary to seek the Lord in the Word. God can easily cease to be the object. His character can be replaced by some "felt need." Some would be insecure without a particular religious movement to follow. Alumni of a Christian school may assume that loyalty to their alma mater is synonymous with loyalty to Christ. Not a few Christians get their best "blessings" from a CD of Christian music or sermons on Christian radio. Take what limited benefits you can from any other source than Christ, but be sure there is nothing more significant to you than feeding your soul on the Lord served best on the plate of the Word.

Manna in the Wilderness[7]

God provided grace for Israel in the wilderness, and He does the same for us in our wilderness experiences. In his sermon on Exodus 16, Dr. Stewart Custer provides the following helpful parallels.[8] Israel's exodus from Egypt and crossing the Red Sea might be compared to our conversion. And their wilderness journey relates to our pilgrimage to heaven. Many Christians are surprised to discover that their path is through a desert (Ex. 16:1). This world is no "friend to help us on to God." It is a place of deprivations, pain, and suffering. As we "hearken to the voice of the Lord . . . and do that which is right in His sight" we do not suffer like the unsaved around us (Ex. 15:26), but "in the world ye shall have tribulation" (John 16:33). We need to remember that conversion is not God's ultimate goal for his people. It is but the first step to being "conformed to the image of his Son" (Rom. 8:29). God "tested" Israel (Ex. 15:25, 16:4), and He "tries" us (Jas. 1). God uses the "trying of your faith" to start the maturing process.

Israel wasn't interested in having their faith increased, so they "murmured" (Ex. 16:2). They all had joined in the "Song of Moses" (15:1-19) to praise God's faithfulness in delivering them from Pharaoh's army. But only three days later (15:22) they began protesting their circumstances. They did not trust the God that controlled the Red Sea to provide enough water to drink! God gave them sweet water, but they failed that test (15:25). A few weeks later He let their food run out. But instead of looking to God, they whined, like we often do. It seemed rational to them to depend only on what they could see and what they could produce themselves. Self-reliance is the enemy of faith. And God will not allow a self-confident spirit in His people to persist. It seems to be his pattern to remove those idols of the heart until we trust His sufficiency alone. Israel failed this test, too.

In verse 3 their complaining was so intense that they esteemed slavery in Egypt as better than their present circumstances under God's care. They totally ignored God and His promises and impugned Moses and Aaron's motive, suggesting that they brought all these people out here to kill them! But, God did not abandon them nor judge them for their unbelief yet.

Again, before any repentance, God miraculously provided. He procured for His people "bread from heaven" (4). Food is important to survive! In other environs they could have produced their own food, but not in the wilderness. There was no garden for them in this wasteland. Jehovah was their only possible source.

Jesus is our "bread of God . . . which cometh down from heaven" (John 6:32-35). "He that cometh to me shall never hunger," He said. All others will. The present tense is used here indicating the need to continually come. Many of us have learned the hard way that when we trust in any other source, we discover that sand cakes don't taste like manna from heaven! Augustine's idea fits here also, "Thou madest us for Thyself, and our heart is restless, until it repose in Thee."[9] A restless, unsatisfied spirit is the mark of the believer who does not feast on "the true bread from heaven."

But why all these tests? First the water; now food is the issue with special instructions for gathering. Was God trying to expose what was in their hearts. He already knew their hearts. He wanted them to know themselves. It was an opportunity for them to see their distrust and to exchange it for trust. Initially the Lord overlooked their distrust. At Kadesh, when the entire nation chose the majority report of the 10 spies, the hammer fell (Numbers 13-14). Every adult over 20 except the families of Joshua and Caleb would die in the wilderness and never see the promised land—all because of distrust.

In God's provision for Israel, He inserted another test for them. He required them to gather daily as much as they needed (Ex. 16:4b). The bread would not keep over night except that which was collected on the eve of the Sabbath (v. 5). Having fellowship every day with Christ in the Word is the parallel for us. The Word is the catalyst for the believer's personal holiness. We cannot spiritually prosper for a single day without that infusion of life. To assume that we can make it today ourselves is to abandon Christ, to take the first step toward "shipwreck" (1 Tim. 1:6), and to move closer to being a "castaway" (1 Cor. 9:27).

Dr. Custer says that "sustaining grace is only from this Book." The Christian lives in a wilderness. The nature of man is such that if we did not have the constraints of difficulties we probably would not trust Christ. I'm sure I would not look "to Jesus, the author and finisher of our faith" (Heb.12:2) if I was not reminded that my faith needs some finishing!

The Berean believers will forever be known as "more noble . . . in that they received the word with all readiness of mind, and searched the scriptures daily" (Acts 17:11). When we see Jesus in the Word, our response will agree with Cleopas and a friend: "Did not our heart burn within us, while he talked with us by the way, and while he opened to us the scriptures?" (Luke 24:32). Jesus Christ is the essence of all the Bible. I wish I could have heard the risen Savior "beginning at Moses and all the prophets . . . expound unto them in all the scriptures the things concerning himself' (Luke 24:27). To talk with Cleopas about that is on my "To Do" list for heaven.

Not only did God's provision keep Israel from starving that day, but also manna sustained them daily for forty years (Ex. 16:35). God's grace is sufficient for the long term. Many believers overlook this simple truth. And the religious industry is quick to fill that perceived need with seminars, books, tours, music, etc. If we filled our heart with "the living bread" (John 6:51), we would not need the wares of the religious entrepreneur. Evangelists and pastor/teachers are God's gift to the Church to equip the saints (Eph. 4:11-12). But the only source for life we have is God Himself through the Word. The youth of Israel daily ate the bread provided them by God. And thereby they succeeded in their journey to the promised land.

The most important thing in your life as a believer is daily friendship with the Lord. The Word of God is the catalyst for that camaraderie. We might wisely come to the Word for many benefits, but the most important is to experience God. Ones purpose in opening the Book will determine his discovery. In the Bible there are many sermons, Sunday School lessons, ethical answers, social solutions, songs, etc. However, our primary purpose in coming to the Word is to see Jesus. John wrote purposefully to help us "believe that Jesus is the Christ, the son of God; and that believing ye might have life through his name" (John 20:31 and 1 John 5:13).

The Word is so important to the believer's friendship with Christ that, if we neglect it, we desert Him. Daily success or failure is marked by what we have done with the Word. When in our pride we assume we can live this day without the Word, we have chosen independence instead of dependence, ostracism from God's direction, and certain failure. No one can read Psalm 119 without seeing the absolute necessity of the Word for the believer. I can testify that in the days I have walked with the Lord in the Word, He has strengthened me (Ps. 119:28), and He will do the same for you.

---

[1]McCheyene, *Memoirs of McCheyene,* p. 267
[2]W. Graham Scroggie, *A Guide To The Psalms,* Vol. II, p. 169
[3]Ibid. p. 175
[4]Andrew Bonar, *Memoirs of McCheyne,* p. xx of the Biographical Information by Andrew Bonar
[5]McCheyne, Ibid., p. 16
[6]Ibid., p. xix
[7]John 6:48-58
[8]Dr. Stewart Custer tape, "The Wilderness: God's Provision"
[9]Augustine, Ibid.

CHAPTER 4

The Relation of Obedience to Friendship

Since friendship with Christ is the most important thing in the believer's life, those who are Christ-focused want that fellowship and want to obey Him in all things. The Holy Spirit living within incites that desire and would teach us that obedience to the will of God is the result of God's ability; not ours. "For it is God which worketh in you both to will and to do of his good pleasure" (Phil. 2:13). However, the tendency in us is to try to follow Christ from our own store of ability.

Many new believers start out with a flurry of energy to serve God and with confidence that *they* can do it. Unless they are soon taught that Christ alone is to be their source they will inevitably discover that the well of self-dependence is shallow. When it is assumed that obedience is within our purview failure is followed by frustration. And disappointment and discouragement are not far behind.

Problem

In almost every other realm of life the objective is the result of our efforts. If the work goals are to be met, I've got to establish what I want to accomplish, plan the work, and work the plan. To get better at a sports activity I must pay a price to train my body to excel. To communicate through a musical instrument I must practice. It may be easily assumed, therefore, that one's relationship to the Lord is also dependent on human ability. Many of the unsaved believe that they are acceptable to God because of their good works.

Many who have been saved by grace think that now they must perform to please God, but the ability to serve God is something given, not something achieved.

Distinction

"Yield-power" is stronger than "willpower." By yield-power I mean that energy that comes from God when the believer is abiding in Christ. By willpower I mean that willable dependence on our abilities. Yielding our spirit to the Lord is effective; whereas, trying to muster willpower from within is ineffective.

There are many passages that remind us of our responsibility to obey God in every area of life. John 12:24-25 tells us how to do that.

> Verily, verily, I say unto you, Except a corn of wheat fall into the ground and die, it abideth alone: but if it die, it bringeth forth much fruit. He that loveth his life shall lose it; and he that hateth his life in this world shall keep it unto life eternal.

The key to bearing "much fruit" is learning how to die. Jesus was to die physically on the cross. He was the "grain of wheat" (NASV) that was to "fall into the ground and die" (v. 24). Verse 25 applies Christ's attitude to us. "Whoever loves his life loses it, and whoever hates his life in this world will keep it for eternal life" (ESV). We are to be constantly "delivered unto death for Jesus' sake, that the life also of Jesus might be made manifest in our mortal flesh" (2 Cor. 4:11). The question for us is "how do I die daily to self?"

Joseph Thayer defines the will as "what one wishes or has determined shall be done."[1] Scripture does not elevate man's willpower; though our culture does with such expressions as: "You can do anything you want to do," and "Where there's a will, there's a way." This attitude certainly does not apply to our spiritual quest. Nevertheless there is a strong contingent of believers who are persuaded that their success is dependent on their will. This opinion easily allies itself with what has been called a "performance-based" sanctification. This view has a list of dos and don'ts, which may differ from group to group, that determines and measures spiritual growth and maturity. With those expectations, we often depend on ourselves to comply. The issue here is not whether certain activities are right or wrong but the source for compliance. I have heard many performance-based messages that end with concrete demands, but with no mention of any aid in obedience. Preaching the Bible is not always preaching Christ!"

Willpower Failure

There are three reasons why I am convinced that human willpower is insufficient to succeed in the spiritual realm. First, spiritual performance is not dependent on desire. Paul itemized lessons he had learned by his own personal failures (Rom. 7:17-23). He had learned that nothing in him was good enough because of indwelling sin (vv. 17, 20) including his will (vv. 18, 21). He learned that in spite of good intentions his actual performance was in the opposite direction (v. 19). He learned that his "delight in the law of God" (v. 22) was trumped by a stronger force; i.e. his flesh (v. 23).

Paul knew from experience that the titanic struggle between the believer's flesh and godly desires is always won by the flesh (Gal. 5:17) unless there is an outside source. Only believers who "walk in the Spirit" have any success over the "lust of the flesh" (Gal. 5:16). All of us who have been "on the battle field" for a while are sadly aware that we always fail when we function independently of the Lord. Satan's power is in alliance with our flesh "to keep you from doing the things you want to do" (v. 17, ESV).

Many believers are discouraged even though they have wanted to and honestly tried to please the Lord. Failure preceded guilt, frustration, and disillusionment. Many will no longer allow themselves to get excited about serving the Lord. Some even drop out of church. At one time they really wanted to make a difference, but discovered they couldn't do it by themselves. Spiritual performance is not dependent on desire.

This discouragement is fueled by religious leaders who get between the sheep and their Shepherd. The job of the pastor/teacher is to point to Jesus—not to enroll a following for himself. Sometimes we "under-shepherds" get in the way of our people getting to Jesus by elevating our opinions higher than humility allows. Dr. Bob Jones, Sr. used to say, "If you can get them to Jesus, they'll be alright!" Success in the pulpit and the pew results from the ministry of our wonderful Priest, not our desire for success.

Second, nothing of spiritual permanence originates in man's will. The Biblical pattern is that everything spiritually significant originates with God and must be powered by Him. God controls all circumstances that touch every believer. He "works all things after the counsel of His will" (Eph. 1:11, NAS). God incites holy desires and empowers them (Phil. 2:13). No one is saved primarily by his choice or decision to accept Christ. For we were born again "not . . . of the will of the flesh, nor of the will of man, but of God" (John 1:13). Scripture "came not by the will of man, but holy men spake as they were moved by the Holy Ghost" (2 Pet. 1:21). Nothing of spiritual permanence originates in man's will.

Third, if anyone could have succeeded as a result of his own willpower, Jesus could have. Yet, He taught and demonstrated that success comes from another supply. Jesus as a human neither determined to make the decisions (John 5:30, Hebrews 10:7-9) nor lived by the power that was His as God. Jesus' life was marked not by self-dependence, but is summarized in John 8:29: "I do nothing of myself."

> Christians are as He was, cast utterly upon the enabling power of the Spirit. The New Testament asserts throughout that Christ lived and wrought on a principle of dependence upon Another. No attentive student can fail to observe this truth (Matt. 12:28; Mark 1:12; Luke 4:14, 18; John 3:34).[2]

Enabling

If willpower is ineffective in obeying God's expectations, how can we please Him? There is a divine enabling for every friend of Jesus.

God requires that we obey His Word. We are responsible not only to choose His will but also to do it. And we will be held accountable for our performance. The problem arises soon after we try to do that without His enabling. If we recognize the disabling force of the flesh, we are ready to move from the Spiritless Romans 7 to the Spirit-dominated Romans 8.

The weakness of the flesh as demonstrated by the Old Testament economy (Rom. 8:3a) cannot be improved upon by the energy of the flesh of New Testament economy believers. It was this same inability of the flesh that doomed the Old Testament law, so "God (sent) his own Son in the likeness of sinful flesh and for sin condemned sin in the flesh" (Rom. 8.3b). By His death on the cross, Jesus dethroned "sin in the flesh" as per Romans 6:1-14.

We must "know that our old self was crucified with him" (Rom. 6:6, ESV) and still "is crucified" (KJV). We must not only know the fact, but also "reckon ye also yourselves ("consider yourselves" NAS) to be dead indeed unto sin, but alive unto God through Jesus Christ our Lord" (Rom. 6:11). And we must "yield" ourselves ("present yourselves" ESV) "to God" and all our parts "as instruments of righteousness unto God" (Rom. 6:13). Musical instruments don't play themselves!

> Many people seem to think that, while unconverted sinners have no power against sin, believers in Christ Jesus have; that is, that God gives to the new-born soul strength in itself to overcome the force of indwelling sin. According to this idea the teaching of the New Testament is "justification by faith" and "sanctification by struggle." But this is an utter mistake, and often proves disastrous to the peace and progress of the soul. Many believers are struggling against sin in the idea that God expects them to "fight the good fight" against evil, but they forget that it is "the good fight of *faith*," and their struggling is very largely in their own strength and inevitably results in failure. God does not give even the believer inherent power over sin. This is not His way of deliverance; His method is altogether different, for He Himself becomes the power dwelling in us that overcomes sin. Not, therefore, by our own struggling, but through the mighty energy of the Holy Spirit within us are we enabled to overcome the power of inbred and indwelling sin.[3]

Yieldedness is not passive, but an active focus on God rather than on ourselves. Obedience not preceded by a yielded spirit is done in the flesh. That might cover a lot in our churches today. But the sacrifice that is brought to God with a "broken and a contrite heart" always scores with God (Ps. 51:17). The beginning of obedience from the human perspective is a yielded spirit to the God of the Word.

---

[1]Joseph Thayer, *Thayer's Greek-English Lexicon,* p. 285

[2]Lewis Sperry Chafer, *Systematic Theology,* Vol. V. p. 80

[3]W. H. Griffith Thomas, *St. Paul's Epistle to the Romans,* pp. 206-207

CHAPTER 5

Help of the Holy Spirit in Friendship

In preparing the disciples for His ascension back into heaven, Jesus encouraged them by emphasizing the new role of the Holy Spirit for them (John 14-16). Paul does the same thing in Romans 8 about which Scroggie writes, "More is said in this portion about the Holy Spirit than anywhere else in the New Testament, except in our Lord's Upper Room Discourse."[1] The Holy Spirit is the agent of personal holiness for every believer. We cannot fully understand the dynamics of spiritual life that we enjoy in Christ, but we can with joy praise Him for the Holy Spirit's hands-on help every day.

We need His help. Satan is plotting to destroy us (1 Pet. 5:8) and uses as many opportunities as he can such as temptations, demons (Eph. 6:12), difficulties, and sometimes people. But his most effective weapon against us is already in us. "Flesh" in the New Testament sometimes refers to the physical. Often the word relates to the spiritual nature in every human that "is hostile toward God" (Rom. 8:7, NAS). It is a family trait of all of Adam's descendents, so it is sometimes called "Adamic nature."

It is also called the "old man." The unsaved have but this one nature, the sin nature. The saved have two natures by virtue of the life of Christ we received at conversion.

We would be in an impossible position in spite of our new birth were it not for two things. First, that fleshly nature in us has already been conquered by Jesus' cross (Rom. 6:1-11). And second, the Holy Spirit now lives in us to help us.

Romans 8 itemizes a partial list of the Holy Spirit's intentions for the believer. The New Testament emphasizes the importance of the ministry of the Holy Spirit in our everyday life. We could not have fellowship with Christ without His help. He is the matchmaker, the facilitator, the enabler.

Rescues

For the law of the Spirit of life in Christ Jesus hath made me free from the law of sin and death (2 Rom. 8:2).

No one can have friendship with Christ while walking in sin (Isa. 59:2, 1 John 1:6).

1 John 1:7 tells us that by walking in the same light "as he is in the light," we can have fellowship with Him, and be continually cleaned from sin. This has been called "preventive cleansing" whereas 1 John 1:9 is "reactionary cleansing." Some people keep their house clean; others clean it after it gets pretty bad! After we have sinned we need 1 John 1:9, and I'm personally glad it's there. But how much better it is to let the light of the Word keep us clean before we mess up!

The Holy Spirit uses the Word to daily keep us clean. The "law of the Spirit of life" (Rom. 8:2) frees us daily from the power of sin in the flesh as per Romans 6:1-11. We were joined with Christ in His death, burial, and resurrection. This is not water baptism but that reality of which water baptism is but the picture. As certainly as we died with Him we have His resurrection life. Christ's death conquered our sin nature (Rom. 6:6).

Resurrection life daily "works for us" as the "law of the Spirit of life." The Holy Spirit is the force that effects our victory over sin. He rescues us from ourselves. Without that help we could not have any fellowship with the Lord due to our constant sin.

Fulfills

The Spirit's ability to rescue us from our negative flesh is a prerequisite for a wonderful, positive function.

"That the righteousness of the law might be fulfilled in us who walk not after the flesh but after the Spirit" (Rom. 8:4).

The "righteous requirement of the law"[2] is that we must "love the Lord thy God" and "thy neighbor as thyself" (Matt. 22:37, 39). Paul agrees that "love is the fulfilling of the law" (Rom. 13:10, ESV). These and other Biblical principles that we are required to obey are to be "fulfilled *in* us," not *by* us. This verb is in the passive voice in the original. As we yield our spirit to the God of the Word, the Holy Spirit gives us energy to "walk not after the flesh, but after the Spirit." This is a wonderful truth! Our daily fellowship with Him in the Word not only feeds mutual communion but also produces "much fruit" (John 15:5). The Spirit fulfills righteousness in us. We need a lot of that help!

Defines

"For those who live according to the flesh set their minds on the things of the flesh, but those who live according to the Spirit set their minds on the things of the Spirit (Rom. 8:5, ESV)."

First in the verse is the negative. Those who set their minds on fleshly things are those who are identified by their sinful nature as either unsaved or a "carnal" believer. But the positive is our focus. Those who set their minds on the Spirit's things are those who live out the Spirit things.

The "things of the Spirit" are a wide category including His interests, goals, methods, and truths. As we "walk . . . after the Spirit" He identifies God's ways, illuminates Christ to us, teaches truth, guides us, and generally keeps us aware of our spiritual environment and needs.

A lot changed when we were saved. We could not know all of it then and we learn more all the time, but we will understand it best when we see the Lord physically.

Our new Father has "delivered us from the domain of darkness, and transferred us to the kingdom of His beloved Son" (Col. 1:13, NAS). Because of this transfer, the believer can no longer be "in the flesh" (Rom. 8:9); i.e. in the "domain" of the flesh. The state in which we now live is "in the Spirit." But we can be "after the flesh" when we "mind," i.e. "think the thoughts of" the world, the flesh, or the devil. We all know that from our own experience. But we can "mind . . . the things of the Spirit," i.e. "absorbing objects of thought, interest, affection, and purpose."[3] The Holy Spirit helps us by describing God and His interests to us as we walk together. He defines reality to us through the Word.

Dwells

"But ye are not in the flesh, but in the Spirit, if so be that (or "since") the Spirit of God dwell in you (Rom. 8:9)."

Because the Spirit of God dwells in the believer, we are said to be "in the Spirit." We are never without Him or His helps. His presence is unconditionally guaranteed for every believer all the time. Therefore, His assistance is always available (John 14:16). He is not the kind of helper that comes sporadically. Certainly "God is our refuge and strength, a very present help in trouble" (Ps. 46:1). The Spirit lives in us.

Champions

"For if ye live after the flesh, ye shall die: but if ye through the Spirit do mortify the deeds of the body, ye shall live (Rom. 8:13)."

Because Christ died to conquer our flesh (Rom. 6:1-11), and the Holy Spirit has the authority and force to make it happen daily (Rom. 8:1-11), our responsibility is to allow "the Spirit" to "mortify the deeds of the body" (Rom. 8:13). This is our obligation but requires His power, because we are completely incapable. He is our champion, Who stands in for us to "put to death" (ESV) the attacks of the already-conquered flesh.

Older believers by experience and observation know all too well how devastating the flesh can be. Our homes and testimonies are vulnerable. Chemical addictions can destroy Christians, too. We need to "be sober" and "vigilant, because your adversary the devil, as a roaring lion, walketh about, seeking whom he may devour" (1 Pet. 5:8). That could happen to any of us, except "the God of all grace . . . make you perfect, stablish, strengthen, settle you" (1 Pet. 5:10). Without help none of us could be successful for a moment. The Spirit is our steady champion.

Leads

"For all who are led by the Spirit of God are the sons of God" (Rom. 8:14 ESV).

All the "sons of God" are "led by the Spirit of God." Every child of God is directed by God, whether or not he knows it. The Spirit conducts us in the way. We are "led by the Spirit" (Gal. 5:18).

The Lord also controls the way. He "worketh all things after the counsel of his own will" (Eph. 1:11). Believing this gives stability, confidence, and assurance. We cannot have consistent companionship with the Lord if we assume that His presence depends on favorable circumstances. If He can only "come over when it's not raining," then He must also be a victim of conditions. If we must control our conditions, we will likely be too busy to enjoy Him. But if He really is in control of our environment, we can rest in Him. The Spirit leads us.

Adopts

"Ye have received the Spirit of adoption, (by whom) we cry, Abba Father (Rom. 8:15)."

The presence of the Holy Spirit brings a new attitude of belonging to God's family. Children in a family by natural birth can rightly envy adopted children. Adoptees are chosen from a large number of possibilities, and often the process requires an enormous amount of money. Adoptive parents must love their children very much.

Believers, too, are adopted. We "are a chosen generation" (1 Pet. 2:9). A huge price was paid for each of us. The Father "spared not his own son, but delivered him up for us all" (Rom. 8:32). Paul was aware of the Roman system.

> The process of legal adoption by which the chosen heir became entitled not only to the reversion of the property but to the civil status, to the burdens as well as the rights of the adopter . . . became, as it were, his other self, one with him . . . We have but a faint conception of the force with which such an illustration would speak to one familiar with the Roman practice; how it would serve to impress upon him the assurance that the adopted son of God becomes, in a peculiar and intimate sense, one with the heavenly Father.[4]

"The Spirit replaces fear with freedom in our relationship to God."[5] What a help this is!

Assures

"The Spirit itself beareth witness with our spirit, that we are the children of God" (Rom. 8:16).

Satan would love to keep us in doubt as to our relationship with our Father. The Holy Spirit bears a strong inward witness to our spirit that we belong to God. In Romans 5:5 the Holy Spirit convinces us of the reality of God's love. Here in Romans 8:16 He convinces us of the reality that we are God's children.

"[T]he 'witness of the Spirit' is the producing of the consciousness of being born of God, of belonging to His family, in Christ."[6]

Notably this witness is not to our minds or emotions but to our spirit. One doesn't need to explain to a child that he belongs to his parents. It is pointless to ask what love is to an engaged couple or to ask why the tear when a patriot sees his flag raised. There are things that one intuitively knows within his spirit.

Does this mean a true believer will never doubt? No. This ministry of the Spirit to His people can be quenched (1 Thess. 5:19). In fact, a believer walking out of fellowship with the Lord will likely doubt. So, why would I choose to live "after the flesh" when I could "fix my heart" (Ps. 108:1) upon the Lord in the Word and enjoy "life and peace" (Rom. 8:6) every day? Assurance is the birthright of every believer, but it must be claimed by faith. It is the Spirit Who assures us.

Intercedes

> Likewise the Spirit also helpeth our infirmities: for we know not what we should pray for as we ought: but the Spirit itself maketh intercession for us with groanings which cannot be uttered. And he that searcheth the hearts knoweth what is the mind of the Spirit, because he maketh intercession for the saints according to the will of God (Rom. 8:26-27).

The Spirit helps us pray effectively. He "helps us in our weakness" (ESV). This weakness (singular in the original language) may point back to our need to wait patiently for God's purposes (18-25) and/or point forward to our ignorance of what to pray for (26b). As we are not left alone in our hopeful waiting (Col. 4:2), so private prayer is not a solo but a duet. "[T]he Spirit lays hand to our infirmity"[7] is Lenski's translation partially fulfilling His job description of being a "paraclete" (John 14:16). The help He offers in prayer is "as if two men were carrying a log, one at each end."[8]

Even when we do pray we often are not aware of many issues involved. We usually don't know the real needs nor what God's intentions are. So, we often pray for the release from every difficulty rather than for the unknown but real needs, which God wants to address by the difficulty. "The trouble is not only our weakness but also our inability to use our great means for obtaining strength as we should. By taking hold with us . . . the Paraclete helps us, indeed."[9]

And, by the way, Jesus helps, too (Rom. 8:34). Along with the Father's welcome (Isa. 65:24), all three of the Trinity are actively involved in the success of prayer, which is the vehicle of friendship. Because of all this help you can effectively pray "in the Spirit" (Eph. 6:18).

If you and I are to have real friendship with the Lord, we need real help. The Spirit is positioned and capable to be all the support we need for that companionship. I am persuaded that many Christians are spiritually discouraged from believing they can be what God wants them to be. The enthusiasm of their conversion may not have been confirmed by biblical discipleship. When their own energy supply was expended they did not know how "to be spiritually minded" to enjoy His "life and peace" (Rom. 8:6). So, after several defeats they retreated into mediocrity convinced that the pleas from the pulpit are beyond their capabilities. If that is you, please learn what is in Rom. 6-8. Do you think you could make it if the Holy Spirit would help you? Well, do I have good news for you! He will! And He is ready, willing, and able now! Don't walk; run to the Lord in the Word!

---

[1]W. Graham Scroggie, *Salvation and Behavior,* p. 53

[2]R. C. H. Lenski, *Interpretation of Romans,* p. 502

[3]John Murray, *Romans,* Vol. 1, p. 285

[4]Merivale, *Conversion of the Roman Empire.* quoted by M. R. Vincent, *Word Studies in the New Testament,* p. 708

[5]Stott, *Romans,* p. 232

[6]William R. Newell, *Romans,* p. 313

[7]Lenski, *Interpretation of Romans,* p. 544

[8]A. T. Robertson, *Word Pictures in the New Testament,* p. 573

[9]Lenski, *Interpretation of Romans,* p. 545

Part Two

Basics for Believers

If information in Part One deals with how to ride a bicycle, Part Two gives the parts of the bicycle. These chapters are more concerned with the basic elements of discipleship than how to do it.

CHAPTER 6

Oneness

In God's mind the believer is associated with Jesus Christ. When the Father sees us He sees the result of Christ's work on the cross. Paul's favorite description in Ephesians of the believer's state is "in Christ." This phrase or its equivalent is used 26 times in the first three chapters. God identifies us with Christ. The Father considers us connected to His Son. He sees us as He sees the Son. Think on that!

God accepts our forgiven status as much as He accepts Christ's sacrifice on the cross. Our future is as sure as Christ's. With our time limitations we look forward to being "glorified" in heaven. But because we are "in Christ," the future is more certain than the past inasmuch as we have difficulty interpreting the past. The Greek tense used in Romans 8:30 indicates that we are already "glorified." "Whom he justified, them he also glorified." This is foundational.

The important words to convey this concept are "one body," "connected," "identity," "attached," "accepted," and "in Christ." W. Graham Scroggie writes, "This identification with Christ is the profoundest truth in the New Testament."[1]

Romans 6

Romans 6 tells us why we can be so confident of our new identity in Christ. First, let's look at the context. Having described the wonderful grace of Jesus in the first five chapters, Paul either anticipates a probable reaction to this doctrine of salvation by grace through faith or directly confronts a known antagonist. The objection to be answered first in this chapter is in verse 1,

"If salvation is so free, then the more we sin after salvation the more grace would be required and God would then be exalted by sin." Verse 2 is Paul's answer in capsule form, which he explains in the next twelve verses. He says it is impossible for anyone to "live any longer" in sin who is already "dead to sin." Essentially he says that when Christ died, was buried, and was resurrected, every believer was effectively with Him. Verse 11 exhorts the believer to accept this truth, and in verses 12-13 to yield to God.

Romans 6-8 is the key New Testament passage on sanctification. The development of these chapters rests on the truth that the believer is one with Christ. We were one with Him in His death, burial, and resurrection. When He died, we died; when He was buried, we were buried; when He was raised, we were raised also. We were with Him!

Water baptism is but a picture of this. The picture is not the reality. I think pictures of the Swiss Alps are beautiful, but that's because I've never seen them! Had I seen them, I would probably say that a picture could never do justice to such an awesome range of mountains. Some think that Romans 6 primarily teaches baptism by immersion. In my opinion there is no water in Romans 6. Oneness is the real thing of which baptism is but the picture. Many of us are far more impressed with the picture than with the real thing. There is something far more important than water baptism in this first paragraph of Romans 6.

This was so important to Paul that he repeats the idea several times. In verse 2, we are "dead to sin." In verse 3, we who "were baptized ('entered') into Jesus Christ were baptized into his death." In verse 4, "we are buried with him," and in verse 5, "we have been planted together." In verse 6, "our old man is crucified with him." In verse 8, we are "dead with Christ." And in verse 11, we are to count ourselves "dead to sin." The magnitude of this truth warrants repetition. When Jesus died, we were with Him in some wonderful way!

This is a big idea and Paul immediately makes the following application. When Christ was raised from the dead, we were raised to life. Look at the several ways he expresses this idea. "As Christ was raised . . . we also should walk in newness of life" (v. 4). "We shall be also in the likeness of his resurrection" (v. 5). "We should not serve sin" (v. 6). We are "freed from sin" (v. 7). "We shall also live with him" (v. 8). We are "alive unto God" (v. 11).

The believer's life is not what we make of it, but is the result of Christ's life. We are one with Him! The fact is that we were with Him then, and the result is that we have His life now. We are one with Jesus!

John 14:20

In John 14:20, Jesus gives in capsule form what the NT letters explain. "At that day ye shall know that I am in my Father, and ye in me, and I in you."

"Ye in me" tells us our position in Christ. "I in you" reveals our source.

> To be 'in Christ' is to be in the sphere of His own infinite Person, power, and glory. He surrounds, He protects, He separates from all else, and He indwells the one in Him. He supplies in Himself all that a soul will ever need in time or eternity.[2]

We cannot get our minds around the idea that God has placed us into the place His Son occupies, but it's true. What a wonderful thought! No other religion has anything even close to this. Only our God could have thought of it and then make it happen.

Hudson Taylor

Hudson Taylor, founder of China Inland Mission, was perplexed. He wrote to his sister, "I felt the ingratitude, the danger, the sin of not living nearer to God. I prayed, agonized, fasted, strove, made resolutions, read the Word more diligently, sought more time for retirement and meditation—but all was without avail."[3]

He wrestled with his spiritual failures for many months. A letter from a friend was used by the Spirit to open Taylor's eyes to the truth of our oneness with Jesus. His friend wrote, "But how to get faith strengthened? Not by striving after faith, but by resting on the Faithful One."[4] (Please read more of Hudson Taylor's discovery in Addendum 2.)

George Muller

George Muller summarizes the benefits that flow to us from this oneness.

> All that we possess in God as His partners may be brought down into our daily life and be enjoyed, experienced, and used. We may make

unlimited use of our partnership with the Father and with the Son and draw out, by prayer and faith, the inexhaustible fullness in God.[5]

The fact that we are joined to Christ is clear in Scripture.

"Who can fathom the depths of the revelation that the believer is related to Christ on the very plane of that oneness which exists between the Father and the Son?"[6]

Our unwillingness to believe it and rest on Him is the root of much of our failure.

The dynamics of this oneness with Christ is where the rubber hits the road. Because we are now in God's family, we have the help we need.

F. B. Meyer

Maybe our greatest need is our daily struggle with our own flesh. F. B. Meyer suggests three steps in the section entitled "How to get rid of the self-life."[7]

1. **He suggests that each of us must first "*consign* my self-life to the cross."**

> For what the law could not do in that it was weak through the flesh, God sending his own Son in the likeness of sinful flesh, and for sin, condemned sin in the flesh: That the righteousness of the law might be fulfilled in us, who walk not after the flesh, but after the Spirit (Rom. 8:3-4).

"Next to seeing Jesus as my sacrifice, nothing has revolutionized my life like seeing the effigy of my sinful self in the sinless, dying Savior."[8]

2. **Second, he says we must *depend* on the Holy Spirit.**

"For if ye live after the flesh, ye shall die: but if ye through the Spirit do mortify the deeds of the body, ye shall live. For as many as are lead by the Spirit of God, they are the sons of God (Rom. 8:13-14)."

The Spirit energizes for the defeat of the flesh and exalts Christ. It is the Spirit who is God's agent in this dynamic.

3. **Third, we must *contemplate* Christ.**

> The one aim of Christianity is to put Christ where man puts self. The Holy Spirit fixes your thoughts upon Jesus. You do not think about self, but you think much about your dear Lord; and all the

time that you are thinking about Him the process of disintegration and dissolution and death of self is going on within your heart.[9]

Note that the power of the cross, the agency of the Holy Spirit, and the believer's focus on Christ is the winning combination. 2 Corinthians 3:18 says this much better than Mr. Meyer or I could.

"And we all, with unveiled face, beholding the glory of the Lord, are being transformed into the same image from one degree of glory to another. For this comes from the Lord who is the Spirit (2 Cor. 3:18 ESV)."

If you are a believer, you are already one with Jesus Christ. Drink deeply of Him, and make much of this wonderful reality until you believe it for every part of your life.

Don't trust your courage or willpower to follow Him. "The arm of flesh will fail you," too. But no believer has learned to trust Him who has been abandoned by Him. Sometimes we don't feel Him any more than a child is aware of or understands his mother from within her womb. But feeling Him is not necessary, being given life from Him is.

---

[1]W. Graham Scroggie, *Salvation and Behavior*, p. 32

[2]Lewis Sperry Chafer, *Grace*, p. 303

[3]Dr. & Mrs. Howard Taylor, *Hudson Taylor*, p. 174

[4]Ibid., p. 168

[5]*The Autobiography of George Muller*, p. 152

[6]Chafer, *Grace*, p. 304

[7]F. B. Meyer, *The Christ-Life for the Self-Life*, p. 39

[8]Ibid.

[9]Ibid., p. 43

CHAPTER 7

Reckon

There are three key words in Romans 6. They are "know," "reckon," and "yield." "The practical, daily, and even momentary use of each of these three key words will give us the secret of perpetual holiness."[1] In the first paragraph of this chapter Paul emphasizes the believer's unity with Christ in His death, burial, and resurrection. Our "oneness" with Christ is something we need to "know" (vv. 3, 6, 9). The following quotation is a repeat from chapter 6, but it's that important. W. Graham Scroggie wrote, "This identification with Christ is the profoundest truth in the NT."[2] God identifies us with Christ. We are benefited exponentially by thinking about our oneness with Him. And it is important that the world identifies us with the Lord.

We come now to the second truth of that triad. The subject matter from Romans 6:1 is victory over the flesh. Every believer has experienced the negative impact of his old nature on his desire to please God. The initial exuberance of the new believer is often forgotten as defeats become common. Having trusted Christ early in their life they get to their high school or college years and decide to go for peer acceptance. Many older believers are persuaded by their failures that the ideal of following Christ closely is not attainable for them. So, they have settled back into mediocrity, of which they are truly ashamed, but from which they see no escape, and for which they have gathered sufficient excuses for their retreat. Romans 6-8 is a key passage for the hungry soul.

Definition

The Greek word translated here "reckon" in the KJV and "consider" in the NAS and the ESV is a favorite word with the apostle Paul being used 27 times in his epistles and only four times in the rest of the New Testament. The essence of the word is to accept what is presented. In Romans 4:3-5, the righteousness of Christ is "counted" to Abraham and to anyone who believes. God credits to our account the very righteousness of Christ (1 Cor. 1:30). So when God sees us, He sees us wrapped in the perfection of His Son. He reckons that to be true. Likewise, we are to reckon ourselves joined to Christ's death, burial, and resurrection. We are to reckon ourselves to be one with Christ.

To "know" is to mentally accept a fact. To "reckon" is to believe that fact with an attitude. William R. Newell explains that "reckon" is "an expression of belief, and of an attitude in view of that belief."[3] This is the step beyond consenting to truth. It is responding to this truth with an inward "yes" rather than "ho hum."

> We are not commanded to become dead to sin and alive to God; these are presupposed. And it is not by reckoning these to be facts that they become factors. The force of the imperative is that we are to reckon with and appreciate the facts which already obtain by virtue of union with Christ.[4]

1 Corinthians 2:12-14 tells us that the Spirit impacts our spirit with truth as Jesus said He would do (John 16:14). Our spiritual response to truth is more important than our mental apprehension.

"Reckon" (KJV) in Rom. 6:11 must not be limited to mentally "consider" (ESV). It must include a spiritual choice and commitment.

Many in their minds do agree to truth whose will is not yet motivated to obedience. To reckon is to stimulate faith. It is the beginning of the obedience of which James speaks; not faith alone, but faith evidenced. Thayer says the verb means "to reckon or account and treat accordingly."[5] In practical terms this is how it works. When I yield my spirit to the God of the Word, the Holy Spirit enlivens the truth of the Word changing my attitude, and my will is kick-started to obey.

This is not a different faith or a different type of faith. The nature of faith is not the focus here but the object of faith. When we were saved, we by faith accepted Jesus' sacrifice for the penalty of our sins. That was easy because we really wanted that long list to be erased. Subsequent to salvation we are admonished to accept Jesus' sacrifice to overcome the power of our sin nature.

This is not so easy because we might not want our sin nature dealt with so harshly. Down deep we like the arrangement of confessing our sins knowing that He will forgive us as per 1 John 1:9. We may prefer to indulge our favorite sin knowing we can get forgiveness rather than leaning on Jesus before we sin.

The difference between the faith required for salvation and the faith required for this commitment is like marriage. Being a groom is easy! But being a good husband is not so easy though it is the same animal!

Appraise Myself Dead to Sin

Paul gives two areas to which this reckoning is to be applied in Romans 6:11. First, we are to count ourselves "to be dead to sin." In verse 1 of the chapter the stated problem is "Shall we continue in sin?" The issue is not whether we have a sin nature. We do and will have it until we are with the Lord. The matter before us is how can I "walk in newness of life" (v. 4) in spite of my sin nature. Paul's answer is that we are "dead to sin" (2).

Do you know anyone who has died physically who lives any longer here? The primary idea of "dead" is separation not cessation. When one physically dies, the real person is separated from his body for a while. Likewise, believers are separated from the "body of sin" (6), which is the structure of sin, the power-house of sin within called "dominion" in verses 9 and 14. Every unsaved person is under this "dominion" of sin. But we who are saved have been "delivered from the power of darkness" when we were "translated into the kingdom of His dear Son" (Col. 1:13). Note that the sphere of darkness is characterized by "power." Dr. Bob Jones, Sr. used to say that unbelievers are not sinners because they sin; they sin because they are sinners. They cannot but do so. It is their nature to sin. They are under sin's dominion. But Christ has changed that for us.

There is some debate as to the meaning of "destroyed" in verse 6. Some suggest that it must mean "abolish" as it does in some other places. I don't think our "old man" ceased to exist when we were saved. The meaning of this word here that aligns itself with other passages is "to make inert, to make inefficient,"[6] or to render inactive.

> Since it ("destroyed") is used here of our sinful nature and in Hebrews 2:14 of the Devil and since both are alive and active, it cannot here mean "eliminate" or "eradicate." It must rather mean that our selfish nature has been defeated, disabled, deprived of power.[7]

We do have a sinful nature, but it was defeated by Christ on the cross. "The apostle does not say that sin is dead to us, but that we in Christ are dead to it."[8] Newell boldly adds, "Your relationship to sin is exactly the same as Christ's."[9] This is a thought-provoking truth! Many will not believe it and choose rather to accept their defeat as inevitable. Some even blame God! But if you intend to live for the Lord, you must receive victory over your flesh every day.

The good news is that Christ has already won this victory for us. All of us who are believers have accepted Christ's atonement for the *penalty* of our sins. Will we now accept this victory on the cross over the *power* of our sin? I repeat Meyer, "Next to seeing Jesus as my sacrifice, nothing has revolutionized my life like seeing the effigy of my sinful self in the sinless, dying Savior."[10]

Your sinful nature is not you. It is an alien. That God loves you but not your flesh suggests that He makes a distinction. Unless you see your sinful nature as a thing apart there will be no room for Jesus to get in between you and your felt need to sin. You will continue to try to struggle alone, and you will continue to fail.

Now then it is no more I that do it, but sin that dwelleth in me (Rom. 7:17).

Appraise Myself Alive to Christ

Paul gives a second area to which we are to apply this reckoning. We are to count ourselves "alive unto God' (Rom. 6:11). The root of the word "alive" is "life," which is that spiritual life we have from God. It is the "spiritual flow" of the life of God into the unsaved to redeem them. It is this same life that flows through the believer to change him into the likeness of the Son and to energize our lifestyle.

Be sure this life that you seek is "unto God." The case of the Greek here indicates to or for whom something is done. The object of this "life" is to benefit and glorify God not primarily us! There are many religious motives other than God! This quest is guaranteed to lead you through sufferings and difficulties. If you are only interested in how this will advantage you, you might look more to the "health and wealth" religious salesmen rather than the Bible. This self evaluation can only be done "through Jesus Christ our lord. "In" might be a better translation. Because we are in Christ, we function by Him. He is the active ingredient.

Ask yourself, "Do I have a proactive attitude toward Christ, and against my sin nature? Does my knowledge of truth redirect my lifestyle?" The Church is laden with believers who know truth, but who are not spiritually motivated. They don't have a positive attitude. They have no fire in the soul. They are acceptable according to peer standards and according to themselves, but are empty of any "hungering after righteousness." From this pool comes those who are satisfied with being average, who have no impact on their neighbors, who are easy victims of Satan's schemes, and who grow old and bitter toward God and His Church. Remember, He whose job it is to convict us of sin is also responsible to glorify the Son to His people. We can do nothing to remedy our plight. The only workable advice is to "look to Jesus." Replace your present focus with Christ, (i.e. learn to gaze on Him in the Word). And thereby somehow life begins to flow to all the needing parts.

Take note of John Stott's thoughts on this verse:

> This "reckoning" is not make-believe. It is not screwing up our faith to believe what we do not believe. We are not to pretend that our old nature has died, when we know perfectly well it has not. Instead we are to realize and remember that our former self did die with Christ, thus putting an end to its career . . .
>
> Can a married woman live as though she were still single? Well, yes. I suppose she could. It is not impossible. But let her remember who she is . . . Can born-again Christians live as though they were still in their sins? Well, yes, I suppose they could, at least for a while. It is not impossible. But let them remember who they are . . .
>
> We are to recall, to ponder, to grasp, to register these truths until they are so integral to our mindset that a return to the old life

is unthinkable. Regenerate Christians should no more contemplate a return to unregenerate living than adults to their childhood, married people to their singleness, or discharged prisoners to their prison cell.[11]

---

[1]W. H. Griffith Thomas, *St. Paul's Epistle to the Romans,* p. 173

[2]W. Graham Scroggie, *The Epistle to the Romans,* p. 32

[3]William R. Newell, *Romans Verse by Verse,* p. 223

[4]John Murray, *The Epistle to the Romans,* pp. 225-226

[5]Thayer, *Thayer's Greek-English Lexicon,* p. 379

[6] M. R. Vincent, *Word Studies in the NT,* p. 678

[7]John R. Stott, *Romans,* p. 176

[8]Thomas, *St. Paul's Epistle to the Romans,* p. 169

[9]Newell, *Romans Verse by Verse,* p. 222

[10]Meyer, *The Christ-Life for the Self-Life,* p. 39

[11]John Stott, *Romans,* pp. 179-180

CHAPTER 8

Yield

The third key word in Romans 6 is "yield" found in verses 13-19. In review, we must "know" our "oneness" with Christ; that we are identified with His death, burial, and resurrection. We also must proactively "reckon" this to be true. Now we come to Paul's application for the believer. We see here *how* we are to respond to the Lord.

The supreme sin of man is his desire to be independent of God. This motive prompted Satan's fall, is the not-so-hidden agenda of the unsaved, and is the first step of the believer's sins. Our carnal nature still craves sovereignty, which should be God's alone. Yet lurking behind each breath is the obsession to "do it my way."

Definition

Paul's antidote is to yield all of us and every part of us to God (Rom. 6:13). The word "yield" here means "to present or show."[1] You might refresh your memory of Chapter 4 under "Distinction." This word is used when Jesus was brought to the temple at eight days old "to present Him to the Lord" (Luke 2:22). The same word is used in Romans 12:1 where all believers are admonished to "present your bodies a living sacrifice." Soldiers "present arms" when they hold their weapon before them. The word means *to give up to*, to give over to as in a presentation, and reminds us that we are not to be independent of God in anything.

Jesus Did!

Christ demonstrated this for us throughout His life on earth. Psalm 22:8 describes the coming Messiah as One who "trusted on the Lord." He would "commit all issues to the Lord" is another translation.[2] Jesus "rolled himself on the Lord." This was the constant attitude of Christ toward the Father. He said, "I do nothing of myself" (John 8:28).

In contrast, our primary problem is that we think we can live this day ourselves without His help. If independence of God is the attitude that precedes all other sins, then certainly the disposition of dependence on God is the first cause of holiness from the human perspective. God has made abundant provisions for His people in His love, the cross of Christ, and the power of the Holy Spirit. But God requires submission of spirit before there can be any fruit of holiness in the life.

Hard to Do?

This capacity to yield is exercised by all humans and defines their life. It is not difficult to do for all do it naturally from birth. Paul implies in Romans 6:19 that we are aware of how we "presented your members as slaves to impurity and to lawlessness" (NASB) before we were saved. We certainly didn't think it was hard to give over to the flesh. It is no more strenuous to "now yield your members servants to righteousness unto holiness." The essence of submission is the same. We are all adept at yielding, but it is usually in the wrong direction. When we "walk in the Spirit" (Gal. 5:16), obedience is easy. But when we don't, "the lust of the flesh" makes it very hard.

Some tell me that in their experience yielding to God is not as easy as yielding to the flesh. I respond that the order of submission for the believer in Romans 6:13 must begin with "yield yourself unto God." Before we can present to the Lord particular testings, circumstances, motives, etc., one's spirit must have already presented everything to the Lord. We did this the moment we were saved, but we have turned away from Him. If we are yet clutching the motives and ways of the world, not only is it hard to yield our "members as instruments of righteousness unto God," it is impossible! But if we have already given *everything* to the Lord, it's not hard to give *every thing* to Him. It's straddling the fence that is problematic!

There are only two forces in the universe; God and Satan. In the believer, those powers are the Spirit and our flesh. Man himself is not a third power. We can only be used by the force to which we yield our spirit.

Order of Yieldedness

The first occurrence of "yield" in Romans 8:13 is a present imperative suggesting to cease an action assumed to be in progress. The second time it is used in the verse it is an aorist imperative emphasizing the urgency and necessity of the action.

What are our "members?" Generally the word refers to the parts of a whole. Here it is connected with the capacities of the "mortal body" in verse 12. Paul probably is looking back at the physical lusts of the body and the weaknesses of the flesh and/or forward to everything that can be an "instrument of righteousness" in the second part of this verse. We need to learn to yield to the Lord everything we are, good and bad; all our thoughts, ambitions, words, responses, actions, and the list could go on. Everything that is not yielded to God, is thereby yielded to Satan. Everything we hold to us in independence of God becomes a tool of the flesh.

On being Slaves

Verse 16 heightens the urgency of the matter. We learn three things from this verse. First, there is no third choice. There is no middle ground. Each of us is at any given moment yielded to the flesh or to the Lord. In the big Biblical picture there are but two combatants; God and Satan. Man's significance is only in his identification with either. Remember, we are not a power.

The unsaved may think he is living his own life when he is actually but a "slave of sin" (v. 17—NASB). When we became a Christian, we did not then become a power for God. We are still "slaves," but now "of righteousness" (v. 17—NASB). Though we have the responsibility to serve the Lord we don't have the power. That is given to us as we yield ourselves and then our parts to His omnipotence. Hopefully this will give you some confidence and peace as you preview the battlefield in front of you.

The second thing we learn from verse 16 is that servitude always follows submission. "We are the bond slaves of that to which we present ourselves for obedience."[3] It is impossible for one to have a self-sufficient attitude and serve God. God only accepts the obedience of a worshiper.

The third lesson in v. 16 is that obedience distinguishes. Two categories are listed: "sin unto death" and "obedience unto righteousness." The direction our heart is yielded will always be indicated by whom we obey. Every unsaved person will consistently obey his earthly instincts and is thereby defined. The frustration of the believer is the battle of the remaining carnal nature with our renewed nature in Christ. There would he no relief for us were it not for our champion, the Holy Spirit (Rom. 8:l3).

OT Theme

That God demands an attitude of yieldedness is a dominant Old Testament theme.

- The lord is nigh unto them that are of a broken heart; and saveth such as be of a contrite spirit (Ps. 34:18).
- The sacrifices of God are a broken spirit: a broken and a contrite heart, O God, thou wilt not despise (Ps. 51:17).
- I dwell in the high and holy place; with him also that is of a contrite and humble spirit, to revive the spirit of the humble, and to revive the heart of the contrite ones (Isa. 57:15).
- To this man will I look, even to him that is poor and of a contrite spirit, and trembleth at my word (Isa. 66:2).

In the New Testament this is parallel with being "poor in spirit" (Matt. 5:3). "Abide in Christ" (John 15), "be being filled with the Spirit" (Eph 5:18), "walk in the Spirit" (Gal. 5:16), and "rest" (Heb.4:9) all speak of the this same thing; the believer's primary responsibility to submit to God in order to engage His omnipotence.

Vs. Willpower

There are differences between willpower and "yield-power" (cf. chapter 4). Our society has succeeded with the leadership of those whose strong, type A, choleric personalities who "make it happen." The kingdom of God, however, does not succeed because big people are strong, but because little people through faith find God's strength. Check out the examples in Hebrews 11.

Those believers who follow the world's method of picking themselves up by their own boot-straps will in time become frustrated. God's expectations are far higher than the best of our capabilities.

All of us tend to be cyclical in our following Christ. Valiant attempts are quickly followed by inconsistency, failure, and then discouragement. Willpower is energy depleting; we only have a limited supply. But yield-power accesses unlimited energy from God. Service for God that is not yielded to God is done in the flesh and cannot merit God's approval though many in the church may not know the difference. Even though the world lauds willpower as the primary force for success, the Bible views man's puny willpower as an insignificant factor and could become a trap.

The human heart has the uncanny ability to do religious things while retaining an attitude of resistance to God Himself. Some come to church while mad at God! Others come only for what they can get out of it.

> Contemporary worship is far more egocentric than theocentric. The aim is less to give glory to God than to satisfy the longings of the human heart. Even when we sing God's praises the focus is on fulfilling and satisfying the human desire for wholeness and serenity.[4]

Yield-power, however, accesses unlimited energy from God. Worship that is "in spirit and truth" (John 4:24) is not physically stimulated and is not motivated for emotional feelings. Yielding my spirit to truth seeks only to affirm glory to God.

Yielding always brings His blessing for even insignificant deeds (Heb. 6:10) and those done to the least (Matt. 25:40). The heart that is submissive to God is not passive. On the contrary, his is an active focus on the God of the Word and is thereby energized. The power that comes from yielding is God's response to a spirit that considers Him to be the only recourse.

---

[1]Thayer, Ibid, p. 498

[2]H. C. Leupold, *Exposition of the Psalms,* p. 198

[3]Murray, *The Epistle to the Romans,* p. 231

[4]Donald G. Bloesch, *Christianity Today,* Feb. 5, 2001, p. 54

CHAPTER 9

Meditation

Since the most important thing in the believer's life is daily friendship with Christ through the Word, *how* to do that must be clearly understood. The writer of Psalm 1 understood the significance of the Word. Though he had less of it he profited from it more than many of us.

The blessed person is the one whose "delight is in the law of the Lord; and in his law doth he meditate day and night" (Ps. 1:2). Remember, the Holy Spirit is the agent for personal holiness. The Word is the catalyst. And meditation in the Word is the method by which it happens.

Method

The meaning of the word "meditate" in the Hebrew is "to muse."[1] It is used for a lion growling continually (Isa. 31:4), a cooing dove (Isa. 38:14), and the mourning that follows defeat or death (Isa. 16:7, Jeremiah 48:31). It might be inarticulate, as those who "imagine deceits all the day long" (Ps. 38:12). It may be articulate. "And my tongue shall speak of thy righteousness and of thy praise all the day long" (Ps. 35:28). The common factor is a continual sound.

So, the basic feature of meditation is to speak or review something continually. Biblical meditation always has an object of filling the mind with truth. And it has form, which is our response to the God of the Word. By contrast Eastern meditation, sometimes called transcendental meditation, attempts to empty the mind or free it of any thought process.

The "biblical approach to meditation must not be confused with the Eastern method of seeking interior silence, which is also called meditation.

The Eastern aim of achieving pure awareness without thought and of experiencing mystical consciousness is the basic task of meditation groups."[2]

If Psalm1:2 is the prescription for biblical meditation, "day and night" is the instruction on the container. Joshua 1:8 says the same thing.

> This book of the law shall not depart out of thy mouth; but thou shalt meditate therein day and night, that thou mayest observe to do according to all that is written therein: for then thou shalt make thy way prosperous, and then thou shalt have good success.

"Remember" is a synonym for "meditate." It is an operative word in Deuteronomy. Israel was to remember God's mighty deeds (7:18), God's faithfulness (8:2), and God's past enabling (8:18). They were to rehearse God's words in their heart (6:6-7), in order that the conditions of the covenant made at Mt. Sinai would be maintained and that they would enjoy the blessings of the covenant rather than experience the judgments. God continually remembers His people (Gen. 19:29, etc.) and His covenant (Ex. 2:24, etc.). Israel failed repeatedly partially because she "remembered not" (Ps. 78). God's indictment was "the children of Israel remembered not the Lord their God" (Jud. 8:34).

The New Testament teaches us that we are to "mind the things of the Spirit" (Rom. 8:5,6), which is to think the thoughts of the Spirit by the Word. We are to "reckon" (Rom. 6:11-12); that is to "count, consider, ponder, let ones mind dwell on."[3] We are to "look . . . at the things which are not seen" (2 Cor. 4:18). That's how we can fix our spiritual eyes upon God's perspective. We are to have our "loins gird about with truth" (Eph. 6:14). Truth holds everything else in place. To "know Him" (Phil. 3:10; Dan. 11:32) is to experience God daily through the Word. Biblical meditation always has the objective of filling the mind with truth and is successful only when there is a spiritual response to that truth.

Meditation is a collateral benefit of praying the Scripture. You might review the section in Chapter 1 on "Reading the Bible." First, read the Word. Read it slowly looking for truth, which is Jesus. And read it responsively responding in prayer to each thought like you were in a telephone conversation with the Lord. Second, store a passage in your mind. After you have enjoyed a time of talking with Jesus, choose a phrase or verse from your reading and memorize it. You may want to write it on something to carry with you or photocopy a page from your Bible.

Third, review the phrase or verse often throughout the day. Repeat it orally or in your mind. The Word can become your all-day sucker! Robert Murray McCheyne said that it is the look that saves; but it is the gaze that sanctifies. By taking the "Word of life" with you through your day you can thereby have His company. And fourth, enjoy the worship. Dwell on the ramifications of the truth you are eating, and let the Word become "the joy and rejoicing of (your) heart" (Jer. 15:16). The Spirit will not miss this chance to remind you of other related good stuff! It will be perfectly acceptable to the Lord for you to make up some tune to sing your meditation to Him "day and night."

Better Way

Those who only have the limited perspective of this world follow the only way they know (Ps. 1:1, Rom. 1:21-32). But there is another way; a better way. Psalm 1:2 describes the attitude with which we come to God's Word. "Delight" means to "have pleasure in."[4] The Word can be our greatest satisfaction because it is the medium of our friendship with the Lord. Our objective in coming to the Word may limit our possibilities. If we come to the Word looking only for a sermon, Sunday School lesson, or evidence for an argument, we may find that but that alone. If we come to find the Lord, He will be found (Jer. 29:13). What a wonderful possibility!

We can have the same attitude toward the Word that the writer(s) of Psalm 119 had. "[T]hy testimonies are my *delight*" (24), "I *hope* in thy word" (89), "how *sweet* are thy words" (103), "I *love* thy commandments" (27), and "I *rejoice* at thy word" (162). If we see the Jesus we love in the Word, we love the Book more. "[T]he law of the Lord" to the blessed man of Psalm 1 is "not a troublesome and unwelcome fetter; it is not a set of hard restraints. It is a joy for him to learn and to do the demands of the law."[5]

There are many helps on the market to organize and direct our quiet time of devotions in the Word. If you use someone's system, don't get so busy that you miss what you are there for! There is far more satisfaction in the yielded spirit lighting on the face of our Lord than fulfilling anyone's order—including mine!

Meditating on the Word helps us digest what we have eaten. It energizes otherwise dormant facts. The objective of biblical meditation is not informational. That comes from study. The purpose is relational. It gives consistency to fellowship with the Lord.

How Long?

Some of us have a problem with this "day and night" qualification in Psalm 1:2. We understand the importance of setting aside a few minutes for a "quiet time" to have "devotions" in the Word. Giving God a small fraction of our day is no problem. Giving Him all day and night can be!

One issue here is maintaining that connection with the Lord through the day. Though we may be busy, all of us keep other things in the back of our minds; someone we love, a tune or song, an up-coming week-end activity, or the hurt of a loss. If truth actually is our delight, activities don't erase that. If I never get tired of being with my second best friend, my wife, Pat, why should being with my very best Friend become boring? I still enjoy new things about her, and we see everything in a new light while following Him, and He is not prone to change! "In thy light shall we see light" (Ps. 36:9). Many ideas lend themselves to almost constant application. "I will bless the Lord at all times" (Ps. 34:1) for: a bed to wake up in, indoor plumbing, warm water, toothpaste, food for which we usually start off with a "blessing," sunshine, a job, etc. If God has created all things and controls all circumstances touching the believer, we can bless Him hundreds of times a day! Try it!

"My soul shall make her boast in the Lord" is Psalm 34:2. There is good and evil boasting. The wrong kind boasts of self accomplishments or stuff acquired. The right kind sees the Lord as the source of all that is good in us and around us and credits Him. Now how many times a day could we do that? And there are thousands of verses that make meditation exciting!

Maybe it would be good to stop reading now and open your Bible. Get a truth about our God, think about it, worship Him, and then come back to reading. You will see that you can enjoy the Lord while you are reading or doing other things.

Another issue here is the way in which we view God. If He is our friend, every thing and every one else will have to find their place somewhere back in the line. If He is an imposition, we can easily come up with reasons why this whole thing is impractical. You see, our society assumes that everything is negotiable. Compromise is a well established political and social foundation of our culture. We bring this concept into our relationship with God and expect Him to play the same game. We have trouble with Paul's conclusion that the believer is a slave of Christ (1 Cor. 7:22, etc.).

Are we Really Slaves?

Meditate on the truth that Jesus is Lord (Rom. 1:3, etc.). We who only know of slavery from history only minimally appreciate what this is. Slaves own nothing. If we are slaves, we own nothing. Children think that whatever they have is theirs! They haven't earned it, but they are persuaded "It's mine!" And one might be wise to take care trying to take away what they are convinced is "mine!" Adults are naturally possessive, too!

All our money is His, not just the tithe. Are you ready to agree that "from him and through him and to him are all things" (Rom. 11:36—ESV)? If we are slaves, doing only some things does not satisfy our obligation to God. We are to "do all to the glory of God" (1 Cor. 10:31). Slaves of men at least have freedom of thought. But slaves of God are to "glorify God in your body and spirit, which are God's" (1 Cor. 6:20). It's not just controlling the evil thoughts we have, but "bringing into captivity every thought to the obedience of Christ" (2 Cor. 10:5). So, in this matter of meditation, it's not a few minutes that we set aside, but we are to "meditate therein day and night . . . for then thou shalt have good success" (Joshua 1:8). Obviously this does not mean we are to have only the Word before our mind all day and night. It means that the God of the Word through the Word of God is our constant companion. "Looking unto Him" becomes our default attitude and our thought of choice.

> Many have found the secret of which I speak and, without giving much thought to what was going on within them constantly practice this habit of inwardly gazing on God. They know that something inside their hearts sees God. Even when they are compelled to withdraw their conscious attention in order to engage in earthly affairs there is within them a secret communion going on. Let their attention be released but for a moment from necessary business, and it flies to God once again.[6]

As Lord, God owns everything! That includes us; all of us by creation, and some of us by redemption. Every incident of independence is sin. But we can "give up" to Him. Every person has been created with a spirit whose primary function is to yield. The world yields to the power grid behind sin as easily as flipping a light switch. Believers can yield to God as easily as we have yielded to the world, the flesh, or Satan. Yielding requires absolutely no energy, no talent, no ability, no training, and no willpower. A yielded spirit to the God of the Word is our first cause of holiness. You may not have the personality, training, or background to meet even your own expectations, and are very disappointed with much of your life. But if you have been saved and will yield yourself to God totally, and every part of you as "instruments of righteousness unto God" (Rom. 6:13), you can be everything the Holy Spirit has power enough to make you! And may I say, it's fun to live this way!

Finally, meditating in the Word day and night is the expected goal. But I praise the Lord for His mercy and patience here as elsewhere. I don't know anyone who has reached the goal. I certainly have not. Truth is, I live on the edge every day. There is a daily conflict whether or not I'll even get into the Word. I often forget the Lord more than I remember Him. I hope you will do better, but don't count on it! Count only on His grace and mercy, or you will get so discouraged that you'll quit! We are more suited to failure than success, and the Lord doesn't lose those opportunities to train us. But the key is to focus on Christ; not on being a spiritual giant!

---

[1]Brown, Driver, & Briggs, *Hebrew and English Lexicon of the OT,* p. 211
[2]Peter Toon, *From Mind to Heart, Christian Meditation Today,* p. 10
[3]Ibid., p. 55
[4]Brown, Driver, & Briggs, Ibid., p. 343
[5]Leupold, *Exposition of the Psalms,* p. 35
[6]A. W. Tozer, *Knowledge of the Holy,* p. 82

Part Three

Leading a Disciple

Parts One and Two have centered on your being a disciple of Christ. There is something contagious about a believer who is smiling inside. This daily experience in you will be unappreciated by some and welcomed by others. Christ has a way of dividing people. Whatever your position in society, there are those you can disciple. Part Three is about how to do that. "It is not great talents God blesses so much as great likeness to Jesus."[1]

CHAPTER 10

The Mandate

For All

All believers are to be disciples and should be involved in making disciples of others. The "Great Commission" (Matt. 28:16-20) provides the directive from our Lord Himself that every believer is to disciple others. As a pastor there are two things that are at the top of my priority list and require the most of my time: prepare the Word for preaching (2 Tim. 4:2) and disciple men (2 Tim. 2:2). The pastor's example in discipling as many as he can is the core of the NT pattern of discipleship.

In Matthew 28:19 "The main verb *to make disciples* is an imperative and means more than merely *teach*; it means *to make committed followers* of the Lord."[2] After conversion, the most important thing for the believer is friendship with the Lord. Establishing and maintaining this connection with the Lord is the objective.

Regarding Christ's assignment in Matthew 28, Alford wrote, "Demonstrably, this was not understood as spoken to the Apostles *only*, but to all the brethren."[3] The pastor must be the leader in discipling and teaching others to do so. But every person who leads someone to the Lord should feel the personal responsibility to disciple him/her, where it is feasible. Every husband as spiritual head of his house should be diligent to oversee the discipleship of his wife and children. A home Bible study is a wonderful opportunity to exemplify and teach discipleship.

You may have noticed that I have used *disciple* as a verb and *discipling* as a participle, though neither use is included in my dictionary.[4] I agree that

"We greatly need an English verb 'disciple,' for this passage [Matt. 28:19], and for [Matt.] 13:52 and Acts 14:21 . . . it may be used in religious discourse with great advantage."[5]

For Elders

Spiritual leadership in the local church is the Biblical responsibility of the elders in that church. My intention here is not to make the case for a multiplicity of spiritual leadership in the local church. But if the pastor is the only Biblically designated leader, his personal influence in this arena is multiplied by only one. He must have some help here. Discipleship cannot be done from the pulpit. The best way is one-on-one. I teach a discipleship class every other quarter in our church Sunday School, but it has been my experience that a new as well as a revived believer progresses best with personal attention and accountability.

A successful church is a group of saved sinners who have fallen in love with Jesus Christ. The difference between a Christ-centered church and church-centered church will be distinguished by the focus. Biblical discipleship alone puts the reality of the Lord in a Bible-believing and Bible-preaching church. After all it's about Him!

Each of us can be a personal disciple of Jesus and help others to be so as well. If we are following Him, it's easy to show others how. After all, we are only pointing others to our Friend. Because He is our Lord by creation and salvation, we believers will also answer to Him in this matter.

For Parents

Many Christian parents wait for others to lead their children to the Lord and feel inadequate to disciple their own. The issue is our own identity. What are we about? What is priority one regarding our children? If we can go through a day and never mention Jesus to our family, we need revival. Only disciples can disciple! If we are full of Christ, it's hard to hide Him!

> 5 And thou shalt love the Lord thy God with all thine heart, and
> with all thy soul, and with all thy might. 6 And these words, which
> I command thee this day, shall be in thine heart: 7 And thou shalt
> teach them diligently unto thy children, and shalt talk of them when

thou sittest in thine house, and when thou walkest by the way, and when thou liest down, and when thou risest up (Deut. 6).

All of us are obligated to obey this "first and great commandment" (Matt. 22.38). To that end "these words" are to be in our hearts by meditation. Parents have the added responsibility to convey this and other truths to their children before they can read for themselves.

Parents can coach their children in truth in a way that establishes and maintains friendship with Christ for them. Here's how.

The class room is home. The class time is any time: when we are sitting with them, when we are walking with them, when we put them down for a nap, and when they waddle in from sleep. That is whenever we can and with diligence. The church cannot do this!

There are three elements involved in teaching children. First, truth needs to be given age-appropriately to them. For my younger grandchildren I start with stories about Jesus. Because Jesus is truth (John 14.6), older children can learn to associate even OT truths with Christ. At the end of the story I ask, "What does this tell you about Jesus?" This establishes the truth. And like a good lawyer never ask a question unless you already know the answer!

Second, ask, "Why is this important?" This emphasizes the significance of the truth. And third, ask, "If you were talking to Jesus, what would you say to Him about this?" Then, if you are alone with them, pray with them about this. This helps them to learn to respond to truth.

The three elements of coaching truth are truth, its significance, and response. Kingdom truth can only be received by child-like people (Luke 18:17). It's hard for adults to become child-like in faith, but it's easy for children. Don't wait! Reference Jesus at every opportunity!

---

[1]McCheyne, *Memoirs of McCheyne,* p. 95

[2]Stewart Custer, *The Gospel of the King*, p. 411

[3]Henry Alford, *Alford's Greek Testament,* Vol. I, p. 306

[4]Webster's New World College Dictionary, p. 410

[5]John A. Broadus, *An American Commentary of the New Testament,* Vol. I, p. 593

CHAPTER 11

The Objective

A disciple follows Christ. Jesus called His original disciples to be with Him. To be with Christ now is the best that is possible for humans. Thinking about the law of the Spirit this moment freeing us from the law of sin and death (Rom. 8:2) makes one smile from the inside out! When one walks with Jesus in the Word not only is there this attitude change but also the many principles of the Bible become more indicative and less subjunctive, i.e. they become more real.

So, the clear objective is Christ. The person you are discipling must learn how to look at Jesus. The best way to make that impression upon him/her is for you to live it. In the real world the Lord uses people who display Christ more than He uses sermons. We encourage our people to advertise Christ more than our church. Hopefully this chapter will impress upon you the centrality of Christ in God's over-all plan.

Substitutes

Alternatives to the simple goal of knowing and walking with Christ via the Word abound. Biblical Christianity is Christ-centered. The most popular substitute for Christ in our religious culture is performance. When Christ is assumed rather than cherished, He becomes the titular head only. His replacement is often a rote recital of do's and don'ts. The difference between being Christ-centered and performance-centered is one's source. On whom is our final dependence? Do *we* do it, or does Christ do it in us?

As you lead a disciple to follow Christ, the type of leadership you provide is important. I think the best model is a player-coach. The example of a CEO, teacher, or even mentor lack the quality of doing what is expected of others. The coach who actually plays with the team is a good pattern for us. Hunger for God is stimulated by example more than anything else. You walk with the Lord, and some will follow, though maybe at a distance. Others will notice and maybe inquire. But don't spend the bulk of your time on those who are not hungry for God. Many professing Christians are not aware of or reject friendship with God. They may actually not be saved, or maybe they can't see in us how attractive Christ really is.

Our Goal

All of us are prone to be led astray "from the simplicity that is in Christ" (2 Cor. 11:3). Religious leaders as well as elements of the world conscript us to follow after them "and not after Christ" (Col. 2:8). Christ alone must be our focus.

Since Christ is head of the Church (Eph. 1:23, Col. 1:18), it follows that we should "grow up into him in all things" (Eph. 4:15). To be a Christian is to be a "Christ-like" one. When the Christ of the Word is the object of our desires, we are motivated to "go forth therefore unto him" who is "without the camp" (Heb. 13:13). A checklist neither makes Christ our head nor separates us from the world.

Some use the name of Jesus only as a mascot for an agenda that is not Biblical. Some become emotionally attached to the idea of Christ, but not to the Christ of the Word. To them love is only an emotion rooted in their cultural imagination—a social reinforcement instead of a personal quest.

The Bible defines and limits Christ. An unbiblical cause using the name of Christ is still unbiblical. The only way to love the real Christ is to love what the Bible declares about Him. The only direction that follows Christ is as per the Bible. Jesus is truth (John 14:6), and the Bible is truth (John 17:17). Both convey the essence of the Father. Spiritual life flows from the habit of fellowship with Christ in the Word. When we neglect the Word, we have discarded Christ. And the frequent, emotional use of His name will not change that.

Christ is the goal because He is the personified wisdom of God. And because of that He is our "righteousness, and sanctification, and redemption" (1 Cor. 1:30). These are the effects of God's plan for humanity in Christ (v. 24).

Biblical wisdom is "insight into the true nature of things."[1] The dynamics of the Church are centered in Christ. The closer we follow Him the clearer our reflection of Him.

"So that the manifold wisdom of God might now be made known through the church (Eph. 3:10, NAS)."

Christ is the goal because He can dwell in our hearts (Eph. 3:17a). This is the first effect of the Spirit's impact on the inner man (v. 16) as we fellowship with the Christ of the Word daily. The second is in vv. 18-19. Every believer is indwelt by the Spirit of Christ (Rom. 8:9), which is tantamount to Christ being in us (v. 10). But not every believer enjoys the manifest presence of the Lord (John 14:21-23). On this passage, Gerhard points us away from subjectivism to the objective Word.

"That is a salutary, practical manifestation of Jesus Christ when he implants spiritual motions into the hearts of his believers and lovers."[2]

This is the best goal for any believer who qualifies.

Christ is the goal because He is the "perfect man" (Eph. 4:13) to Whom we aspire. Our ultimate purpose is conformity to Christ. Individually and collectively we will be presented to the Father as the bride of Christ "holy and blameless and above reproach before him" (Col. 1:22, ESV). The means to that end is that we focus on Him, and somehow God changes us "into the same image" (2 Cor. 3:18). Change is sometimes hard. But here it is not hard to do because we don't do it. He changes us!

The performance-centered believer is motivated by other goals, and will not progress as a disciple. Christ can be assumed in the context of church activity and numerical growth. But ours is a jealous God Who will have no other goals before Him. All believers know about Him, but few are motivated to know Him. Your job is to stand with the disciple in their experiences and encourage them to look to Jesus Who alone is "the author and finisher of our faith" (Heb. 12:1).

Our Measure

That believers have been predestined "to be conformed to the image of his Son" (Rom. 8:29) states both the ultimate goal and the intermediary measure. Predestination guarantees it will happen; conformation measures the daily progress. On Ephesians 4:20-21 Moule writes that Christ "is the subject matter of His own message."[3] Christ is our standard. In class we study the subject over which we are to be tested. How well we learn the information becomes the measure of our grade except for those "trick" questions! To prepare for the test study the subject. Jesus is the measure for the Christian, because He is the subject of our new life.

Jesus displayed His deity by manifesting the power (John 3:2), the wisdom (John 7:46), and the glory (2 Cor. 4:6) of God in ways we cannot duplicate. But He also showed us qualities of God we can replicate. Christ and the writer of the NT challenge us to be like Him. In this sense Jesus is the measure of the Christian life. Everyone follows some model, whether we know it or not. The world has their models; we have the best!

Jesus is our example in suffering (Col. 1:24). Lightfoot summarizes Paul's thought here.

> I, Paul, the feeble and sinful, am permitted to supplement . . . the afflictions of Christ. Despite all that He underwent, He the Master has left something still for me the servant to undergo. And so my flesh is privileged to suffer for His body—His spiritual body, the Church.[4]

The incarnation, life, and death of Jesus demonstrate how to identify with people for ministry (Phil. 2:6-8). Of course, Jesus' suffering was unique because He is God, but we are to duplicate His mindset in joining those in difficulty (Phil. 2:5). We are to help them in their struggle and sometimes help them out of it while remembering the purpose of needs. Man's purpose is to glorify God and to enjoy Him. Our greatest need is to trust God. He graciously allows and/or designs troubles as the most common opportunity for us to need and therefore trust God. Jesus is the issue, not our pain. He is both our example and our purpose in suffering.

Jesus is our model for progress (Col. 2:7). "In Him" and its equivalents are favorites of Paul. We often read over this phrase with little thought. But being "in Christ" is a deep source for the best meditation. Thayer says it is used . . .

> Of a person to whom another is wholly joined and to whose power and influence he is subject, so that the former may be likened to the place in which the latter lives and moves. So used in the writings of Paul and of John particularly of intimate relationship with God or

with Christ, and for the most part involving contextually the idea of power and blessing resulting from that union . . . [5]

Try meditating on Romans 8:1a for a few days, and you will experience gratitude, love, a positive attitude, and an inner beam!

Jesus is our freedom from being controlled by others (Col. 2:8). People are like scalps on a pole or notches on the gun to many whose success is measured by numbers. Some pastors don't know the difference between their opinion and truth. Through rearrangement and pure deception, charlatans use comfortable traditions and commonly accepted truisms to captivate fans. We all are vulnerable to these were it not for Christ. How do we know we are not being led astray by a personable, knowledgeable wannabe? Paul says the wrong way is "not after Christ." He is the measure. If we don't know how to follow Christ, we really don't know!

Jesus exampled the Father for us. Of the then coming Church age, Jesus said, "I shall show you plainly of the Father" (John 16:25). We are joined to the Father in the Son. Specifically Christ demonstrated for us the Father's love (1 John 3:16, 4:7, 10; John 3:16). Jesus died and lived the love of God as a model for us (John 12:24-25; 2 Cor. 4:11). He also showed us what to talk about (John 8:26), which actions to emulate (John 8:29), and Whom to honor in our life (John 8:49-50). In short, Jesus is the measure of the Christian life, and we can be like Him. The next section details this.

Our Means

Jesus is the way to success because in Him we are complete (Col. 2:10). If success is our being perfect, speaking only right words, knowing everything we need to know, rearing perfect children, having ideal marriages, most of us are in trouble! If success is dependent on our measuring up to God's best, none of us will make it. In verse 9, Christ is the "fullness of the Godhead." In verse 10, believers are "full in Him" (NAS). The words "fullness" and "full" mean more than we have space for here, but for our purposes read "ye are successful in Him." Lightfoot suggests, "Ye are filled from His fullness."[6]

God in Christ gives life freely. Lesser religions require performance. Jesus is the means to life (John 3:16) and to living (Gal. 2:19-20). No informed person would say that our salvation is dependent on us. We know it rests on Christ's finished work on the cross. But many would imply that the life we live after we are saved is primarily contingent on us; on our will power, our obedience, our praying, our choices, our soul-winning, our separation, etc. That is, we are saved by grace but are sanctified by works. However, we are warranted to "Look as much to Him for sanctification as for justification."[7] The issue is not whether or not we are responsible to exercise our will, be obedient, etc. It's a question of distinguishing the cause and the effect. Do we find life from within ourselves, or is Christ the life that produces these effects?

The Bible teaches that Christ is the cause of the Christian life as well as the means of salvation. Our failure in holiness is a matter of unbelief rather than our lack of ability. Paul addressed both salvation by works (Gal. 2:16) and sanctification by works (Gal. 3:3) with the truth that Christ is life.

The issue before Paul in Galatians 2:19b is "that I might live unto God." That possibility is turned into reality in v. 20. As a result of the believer's co-crucifixion with Christ, "I have no longer a separate existence. I am merged in Christ."[8] Now "Christ liveth in me." The believer is "in Christ," and Christ now functions in him (John 14:20). The source of the believer's new life, resulting in obedience, sharing our faith, etc., is now Christ.

Dependence on ourselves to do right is parallel with the Jews' confidence in themselves to keep the law. Looking within for the resources to please God is short-lived, disappointing, and then frustrating. So, many believers quit trying or stick to a more doable, guru-supplied list. This discouraging dualism is addressed by our oneness with Christ. Paul's example is that Christ did live in him and that life is available to all believers "now." For many of us the issue is not informational. A few more years of expository messages will not do what the others have not. The issue is relational.

> Faith means reliance or dependence. The Christian lives by continual dependence on Christ, by yielding to Him, by allowing Christ to live His life in him. Thus the believer's rule of life is Christ and not the law. It is not a matter of striving, but of trusting.[9]

We do not have the power to do what is right. We can only choose which power will be displayed through us. That Christ is our life is one of the hardest truths to convey. The person you are discipling may be preconditioned with other objectives. Many evangelicals are replacing Christ with worldly success. Some groups champion a particular version of the Bible. Others have a Bible teacher whom they follow more closely than the Word itself. We must not assume Christ, while working for our own definition of success. Christ is the only goal, measure, and means for real life. Keep the focus there!

---

[1]Vine quoting Lightfoot, *Expository Dictionary,* p. 678
[2]Lenski, *The Interpretation of St. John's Gospel,* p. 1008
[3]H. C. G. Moule, *Studies in Ephesians,* p. 117
[4]Lightfoot, *Saint Paul's Epistles to the Colossians and to Philemon,* p. 164
[5]Thayer, *Thayer's Greek-English Lexicon,* p. 211
[6]Lightfoot, *The Epistle of St. Paul to the Colossians and to Philemon,* p. 177
[7]McCheyne, *Memoirs of McCheyne,* p. 273
[8]Lightfoot, *The Epistle of St. Paul to the Galatians,* p. 119
[9]William MacDonald, *Believer's Bible Commentary,* p. 1880

CHAPTER 12

Prerequisites

Discipleship only occurs as the disciple becomes more attached to Christ in the Word.

If you are doing the discipling, it is important to remind the disciple that Jesus is the object, not outward religion. The expectations of many, including the disciple, may be other than real friendship with Christ. The following three qualities are necessary for long-term success.

Saved?

First, is this person saved? "Learner, pupil, apprentice, adherent" are synonyms for the noun "disciple."[1] A disciple is one who has faith in Christ. Certainly one does not become a disciple because of or at the moment of outward baptism as suggested by Lightfoot.[2] No ceremony can effect a spiritual change or even date the beginning of that change. The importance of ritual baptism is more in the truth it conveys than in the ceremony itself.

The leader needs to know as much as humanly possible that this person in fact knows Christ as their Savior. It is true that all believers are categorically disciples by virtue of faith in Christ. In Acts, the term is used of all the Christians (6:1-2, 7; 14:20, 22, 28; 15:10; 19:1, etc.). But in John a disciple is qualified by the Word (8:31), love (13:35), and fruit (15:8). So, only Christians can be followers of Christ, and we all can be better disciples.

Some have come to a saving knowledge of Christ during the process of discipleship. This should be the exception. And we should not begin discipling them before we are confident they are saved just as we would not baptize anyone before salvation. If we attempt to disciple an unsaved person, we run the risk of confirming them in their unbelief. When an unsaved person gets comfortable in church and in his mind misapplies Biblical terminology, he becomes more insulated from the Gospel. So, as much as you can, inquire and watch before you begin.

Hungry?

Second, do they have a hunger for the Lord? This is not always easy to determine initially. But you'll know soon! Jesus said that the then-coming Holy Spirit "shall glorify me" (John 16:14). This is a wonderful and fascinating ministry of the Spirit in each believer. Jesus is "life" (John 14:6), and the Holy Spirit makes that life actually live in us. An often-used metaphor for this phenomenon is food and our physical need for it. "Blessed are they which do hunger and thirst after righteousness: for they shall be filled" (Matthew 5:6). The Holy Spirit creates that divine hunger for the reality of Christ. Suddenly, and almost without reason, the satisfactions of the world taste like spoiled milk! When "the Spirit of truth" glorifies Christ before us, we lose our appetite for everything else. Somehow Christ becomes more interesting than TV!

The new convert will usually have this excitement about Christ. When older believers are revived and walk in fellowship with Him, the Spirit draws our attention to the Lord (John 15:26). Actually that's all discipleship is!

Since discipleship is Spirit-directed fellowship with Christ in the Word, there is a danger of mechanically going through the process, when the person is not hungry for Christ. It fosters a hypocrisy in them that we know all too well. When you have a discipleship class open to all, it's hard to qualify those who come. But you can emphasize the importance of the primary goal of spiritually walking with Christ.

Needs?

This third prerequisite to consider before discipling someone is close to that of hunger, but an additional question should be considered, though it may not be easy to answer. Is Christ their main need or are they otherwise motivated? Often a problem marriage, a physical challenge, chemical dependency, or other troubles may be the need that first causes us to seek Christ's help. Certainly He delivers people who are in need. But many whom Jesus fed and/

or healed went away happy but without Jesus. Is the primary desire to follow Christ, or are they only looking for relief now? It has been my experience that those who come to Christ who "labor and are heavy laden" with needs, but who do not "take my yoke . . . and learn of me" (Matt. 11:28-29), will not be "fruit that remains" (John 15:15). Just remember that the purpose here is Christ; not marriage counseling or whatever else may be on the surface.

The first invitation to follow Christ is in the context of needs. We first came to Him because we needed forgiveness of sins. The truth of the matter is that we didn't know how much we needed the salvation He offered. And we still don't know. A consequence of the fall is that man has great needs, many of which we are not even aware. Every day we all have needs; some are unconscious, which only Christ can help by our friendship with Him through the Word.

Man's purpose is to glorify God. Our need for this purpose is to trust God. Suffering is the greatest opportunity for us to trust God for His glory.

God allowed Paul's "thorn in the flesh" (2 Cor. 12) to allay possible pride and demonstrate Christ's sufficiency for Paul's physical need. "It is good for me that I have been afflicted; that I might learn thy statutes" (Ps. 119:71). Afflictions are good for us. "O Lord . . . thou in faithfulness hast afflicted me" (Ps. 119:75). God afflicts His children for good.

Not many would disagree that we have needs. Often we do not seek Christ for the little daily needs like conquering our flesh in selfishness, anger, or stress. But when we find ourselves with serious needs like dysfunctional homes, combative relationships, and general failure in many areas of life, we are more prone to seek Him for answers.

Our sinful nature, though conquered by Christ on the cross (Rom. 6), is yet retained by every believer and causes our greatest need for Christ daily. Most believers recognize that we have needs, yet most believers do not retain Christ daily for their daily needs.

Therefore, God prepares us for Christ by underscoring our need. Most of us came to Christ initially because of our need, and we continue to come partly because we still have needs. Failure is part of the "all things (that) work together for good" (Rom. 8:28). So why does God allow or even create failure in our chastening? It is to set up a struggle between self and Christ.

There are two dynamics at work here. First, the struggle between self and Christ often, but not always, creates hunger for the better. Think about that in the realms of education, music training, and sports. The value of almost anything creates a desire for it. But this is not more self-evident than in the spiritual realm.

"And there is nothing on earth that I desire besides you (Ps. 73:25—ESV)."

Spiritual desire is a prerequisite for spiritual growth and maturity.

God heightens the struggle to make obvious the need so that we will hunger for reality enough to yield our spirit to the God of the Word.

"Come, and let us return unto the Lord; for he hath torn, and he will heal us; he hath smitten, and he will bind us up (Hosea 6:1)."

The second dynamic here is predestination. Election impacts conversion, and predestination impacts sanctification. Predestination is God's road map for each believer "that (eventually) we should be holy and without blame before him in love" (Eph. 1:4).

I must write quietly here lest we get the unwanted attention of the dueling Pelagians and Augustinians! Whatever else predestination may imply to the theologians, there is great comfort for the simple believer in the decree from the Lord that He has positively planned for us to be "conformed to the image of his Son" (Rom. 8:29). To that end He "worketh all things after the counsel of his own will" (Eph. 1:11).

Our needs discovered in our specific circumstances, inabilities, background, destitution, sins, etc., are not greater than the Lord's ability to deliver. I don't think anyone would disagree with the idea that if God wanted to help us with our great need, His help would be decisive. Well, He wants to!

Every successful disciple of the Lord is walking in fellowship with the Lord and is thereby being helped with all his/her needs. But from many troubles the Lord has no intention to free us. The care-free life literally sold by the "health and wealth gurus" is not the Biblical intent. "Casting all your care upon him" (1 Pet. 5:7) does not guarantee that those cares will vanish. In fact, it may be the Lord's design for us to demonstrate that "*in* all these things we are more than conquerors through Him that loved us" (Rom. 8:35-37). Endurance demonstrates more grace than deliverance. Because we are following Christ and are experiencing His deliverance daily, we are prepared to disciple others.

Only walking with Christ qualifies and entitles one to lead others to do the same. We have the most satisfying opportunity to "comfort them which are in any trouble, by the comfort wherewith we ourselves are comforted of God" (2 Cor. 1:4). This is only true if we have been comforted of God. And what kind of a person who has discovered the source of all comfort would not share that in such a needy world?

If you would like to share your source, look for hurting people. Do you know any right off? Are there any in your orbit with marital difficulties, financial problems, chemical addictions, or sickness? This is the best pool for potential disciples. Many outside the church are quite willing to talk of their troubles. They are often far more transparent than church people who have a vested interest in maintaining the impression that "good Christians don't have problems like the world. Everything is perpetually fine." In your normal conversation with people who share a difficulty in their life, you might ask them when alone "would you be interested in knowing what the Bible says about that?" If they say "yes," tell them how Christ meets all your needs and that He can do the same for them. If they say "no," you won't have to endure their complaining any more!

Offer them Christ instead of religion. Don't invite them to church before you invite them to Christ. You can usually direct the conversation to our greatest need of salvation. You may be surprised at how many people in our society have no idea what the gospel is and who really don't mind talking about it.

So, keep in mind how the Lord uses needs to motivate us to come to Him. We need needs! But we need Him more. In fact, He is better than an existence without any human needs. Discipleship is all about Him. Keep in mind that needs are not an end in themselves but are only an opportunity to know Him.

As you think about these qualities in a potential disciple, don't think too much! Recommending Christ to be the Friend of someone is not hard. All you do is point! The real dynamic occurs between them and the Lord. You are only a facilitator and encourager. Please don't let this become an overwhelming task. Love Jesus and you'll have a hard time being quiet!

---

[1]William F. Arndt and F. Wilbur Gingrich, *Greek-English Lexicon of the NT,* p. 485

[2]Lightfoot, *Commentary of the NT from the Talmud and Hebraica,* Vol. II, p. 379

CHAPTER 13

Preparations

Prepare Leaders

The primary preparation for leading a disciple is for the leader himself to walk with the Lord in the Word daily. If the desire is to involve a group of people who will serve as leaders, such as elders, deacons, SS teachers, or parents, it would be helpful if there were meetings with the group to organize the paper-work and to review the procedure. It must also be decided where this will take place; in already established small group settings, in homes or at church, etc. In Addendum 3 is an overview particularly for a youth group.

A discipler's function is to encourage and facilitate the disciple's experience in the Word. Not to deflate an enthused leader, but really we are not absolutely necessary to the process. The goal is for the disciple to learn to eat the Word themselves without the need for someone to put a bib on them and watch them eat! But it's always good to eat together physically and spiritually! We leaders, though, must remember that we are helping them with a relationship with the Lord, not with us.

Prepare Material

Being a disciple with whom our Lord is pleased requires no paper work. It is totally a spiritual thing. But some find it helpful to journal, and many might need the accountability that a written response provides. When written replies are part of the procedure, it is necessary to keep the focus on the spiritual response. Initially, many will want to write down what they are learning rather than their actual response to the Lord. Remember, this is about a relationship and not about information.

We will mention several printed items that may be helpful, and in Addendum 4 and 5 are copies you may freely duplicate and change to your preference. Especially for teens, a Commitment Agreement can be a pledge that is more difficult to forget. Addendum 6 provides the key idea for each chapter for the teacher.

The response record helps write out what is happening inside the disciple. In a typical verse, there are many possible responses to the Lord, but usually one will stand out. That's the only one they need to write down. The goal of the *Responding to Jesus* sheet is to help with three things. First, initially focus on no more than two or three verses per sitting. Second, respond spiritually to the Word in yielded obedience. See *Reading the Bible* in Addendum 4 that we use in brochure form at our church and *Finding Jesus in the Bible,* which is the same thing adapted for teens. Third, memorize a phrase on which to meditate throughout the day. If one is memorizing a passage other than the one they are using for their quiet time, it might be better to meditate throughout the day on something from those verses. I write these verses on a card to keep with me, save the cards in a drawer, and every so often have such a great time reviewing those love-notes.

Prepare Schedule

If this is to be a part of an ongoing small group, SS class, or in the context of a parent with their child, it may be open-ended as to duration. If one is discipling a new believer or a revived believer, meeting with them weekly for a month or two should be sufficient. Keep in mind that the objective is to train them to establish and maintain fellowship with the Lord on their own. If being a friend of Christ is perceived to be a function of the group or the result of the encouragement of a leader, the objective is lost. The most important relationship a believer has is personally with the Lord, then with family, followed by the church, and lastly society. When that order is rearranged, problems ensue, and usually the Lord is forgotten or assumed.

For a typical thirteen week SS quarter, on the 1st Sunday I like to present them with a printed Addendum 4, *Reading the Bible.* Explain it, practice on Ps. 23.1, and assign one verse per day for the next week. Go over their responses at the 1st of the next week's class, and weekly check that they are engaged daily. I have never been able to do a chapter per week. Don't try to go through more than the first nine chapters in a quarter.

Prepare Procedure

The procedure is not the most significant part of this process. The spiritual determines the procedural, not the other way around. However, spiritual leadership requires some *modus operandi* for the sake of both the disciple and the leader.

In the initial meeting with an individual, begin with letting them share their salvation experience and remind them that the same faith that saved us enables us to walk daily with Him (Col. 2:6). Then help them clarify the purpose of your meeting together. I have found that usually the first issue is not distinguishing the mental from the spiritual. The purpose is not to learn what the Bible says. It is to yield one's spirit to the God of the Word. If that distinction is not made, then all you have is a tutored Bible study. As important as studying the Bible is, that's not the purpose here. Getting more information will not help if we are not spiritually yielded to the truths we already know.

Be sure they know your expectations of them in the areas of duration of meetings and method of accountability. If this is a one-on-one relationship, I think it is a good idea to give them an opportunity to back out graciously,especially if you can sense that the desire is not there. It would be better for them to wait until they are prompted by the Spirit instead of the expectations of their leader. It has been my experience that when there is unconfessed sin the Holy Spirit will not even try to glorify Christ to them. For them, He is more involved with chastening and conviction. So, if you allow them to go through the outward process of discipleship, you might be working counter to the Holy Spirit. If you are walking in fellowship with Christ, it's not hard to know who want Him and who are just playing the game.

For subsequent meetings there are three targets. First, and most important, is to let them share their friendship experience with the Lord for that week. What you are looking for is their connection with the Lord via the Word. It should disclose a personal connection to the Lord as they are reading His thoughts. It should indicate submission as they are yielding themselves to Him. And it should reveal a closeness with Christ as they are building a relationship with Him.

Second, briefly answer any questions that may have arisen during the week. Even though the intent is not Biblical education, try to answer the questions you are secure in. Refer the others to someone who might know. But don't let your time together become another Bible study. At first put them in a passage that lends itself to your purpose; not Deuteronomy or Revelation. I like to start them with Psalm 23. Many already have this memorized, and it quickly builds confidence in the Lord's care. If you get questions like, "When did David write this?" or "Isn't He still the shepherd of the Jewish nation?" you can surmise that they are not looking at the Psalm for the right reason. If you get questions like, "Does this mean that the Lord will always provide everything I need?" they are on the right track.

Third, encourage them with your experience of friendship with the Lord. There is nothing that stimulates hunger for the Lord more than an example. Most Christians seldom see anyone daily walking with Christ. Sermons, books, even testimonies cannot replace an up-close sample. If you are not enjoying fellowship with the Lord, you do not qualify to disciple anyone else. In fact, you couldn't if you tried. But if you are simply loving the Lord and walking close to Him, this will be an easy task. Spirit touches spirit. You don't have to teach, impress, or control; just be. You may think you are leading, but mainly you are pointing!

Prepare for Excuses

Everyone will fail the ideal. Accountability will expose several excuses. You and I can afford to be understanding! Yielding one's spirit to Truth is easy; consistency is not. I have never met anyone who has been consistent in their daily walk with Jesus. That awaits heaven. For now remember that a yielded spirit to the God of the Word is the continuing first step. Habit helps, but none of us is there yet. So, without giving them an out, encourage them in the progress they are making.

Here are some of the excuses I have used and heard. "I don't have time." The issue is priorities. "I don't understand what I am reading." Put them in a patch where the fruit is more obvious. "I forget to meditate." Use a cheat-sheet! Keep it with you. Copy the page, write it on a card, or abbreviate the phrase on your wrist! Yea, that's me! "I can't meditate and focus on my work at the same time." Enjoying Christ when we can focus on Him will create a subconsciousness of His presence. His control of our spirit becomes a sweet taste in our mouth, and He becomes our welcomed default setting when we do have a crack of time. "This is too much for ordinary Christians." Abort! They are not ready to begin. Find someone who is hungry.

ADDENDUM 1

George Muller's Testimony

"It was at Nailsworth (in England) that spring (1841) that he began a practice that he never abandoned during the remainder of his life. Up until this time he had made a habit, after having dressed in the morning, of getting straight down to prayer. But while at Nailsworth it came to him that the most important thing was to concentrate first on reading the Bible, meditating on the chosen portion:

> That thus my heart might be comforted, encouraged, warned, reproved, instructed; and that thus, by means of the Word of God, whilst meditating upon it, my heart might be brought into experimental communion with the Lord . . . The first thing I did (early in the morning), after having asked in a few words the Lord's blessing upon His precious Word, was, to begin to meditate on the Word of God, searching, as it were, into every verse, to get blessing out of it; not for the sake of preaching on what I had meditated upon; but for the sake of obtaining food for my soul. The result I have found to be almost invariably this, that after a very few minutes my soul has been led to confession, or to thanksgiving, or to intercession, or to supplication; so that, though I did not, as it were, give myself to prayer, but to meditation, yet it turned almost immediately more or less into prayer . . . With this mode I have likewise combined the being out in the open air for an hour, an hour and a half, or two hours before breakfast, walking about in the fields, and in the summer sitting for a little on the stiles, if I find it too much to walk all the time. I find it very beneficial to my health to walk thus for meditation before breakfast, and am now so in the habit of using up the time for that purpose, that when I get in the open air, I generally take out a New Testament of good-sized type, which I carry with me for that purpose . . . and I find that I can profitably spend my time in the open air, which formerly was not the case for want of habit . . . The

difference, then, between my former practice and my present one is this. Formerly, when I rose, I began to pray as soon as possible, and generally spent all my time till breakfast in prayer, or almost all the time . . . But what was the result? I often spent a quarter of an hour, or half an hour, or even an hour on my knees, before being conscious to myself of having derived comfort, encouragement, humbling of soul, etc.; and often, after having suffered much from wandering of mind for the first ten minutes, or a quarter of an hour, or even half an hour, I only then began really to pray. I scarcely ever suffer now in this way. For my heart being nourished by the truth, being brought into experimental fellowship with God, I speak to my Father, and to my Friend (vile though I am, and unworthy of it!) about the things that He has brought before me in His precious Word. It often now astonishes me that I did not sooner see this point."[1]

---

[1]Steer, George, *George Muller Delighted in God!*, pp. 103-104.

ADDENDUM 2

Hudson Taylor's Testimony

In 1869 a fellow missionary, Mr. McCarthy wrote to Hudson Taylor:

"I do wish I could have a talk with you now about the way of Holiness. As the time you were speaking to me about it, it was the subject of all others occupying my thoughts—not from anything I had read, not from what my brother had written even, so much as from a consciousness of failure; a constant falling short of that which I felt should be aimed at; and unrest; a perpetual striving to find some way by which I might continuously enjoy that communion, that fellowship at times so real, but more often so visionary, so far off! . . . Do you know, dear brother, I now think that this striving, effort, longing, hoping for better days to come, is not the true way to happiness, holiness or usefulness: better, no doubt far better, than being satisfied with our poor attainments, but not the best way after all. I have been struck with a passage from a book of yours left here, entitled *Christ is All.* It says:

> The Lord Jesus received is holiness begun; the Lord Jesus cherished is holiness advancing; the Lord Jesus *counted upon as never absent* would be holiness complete.
>
> This (grace of faith) is the chain which binds the soul to Christ, and makes the Saviour and the sinner one. . . .
>
> A channel is not formed by which Christ's fulness plenteously flows down. The barren branch becomes a portion of the fruitful stem . . . One life reigns throughout the whole.
>
> Believer, you mourn your shortcomings; you find the hated monster, sin, still striving for the mastery. Evil is present when you would do good. Help is laid up for you in Christ. Seek clearer interest in Him. They who most deeply feel that they have died in Christ, and paid in Him sin's penalties, ascend to highest heights of godly life. He is most holy who has most of Christ within, and joys most fully in the finished work. It is defective faith which clogs the feet, and causes many a fall.

This last sentence I think I now fully endorse. To *let* my loving Saviour work in me *His will*, my sanctification is what I would live for by His grace. Abiding, not striving nor struggling; looking off unto Him; trusting Him for present power; love of an almighty Saviour, in the conscious joy of a *complete* salvation, a salvation 'from all sin' (this is *His* word); willing that His will should truly be supreme—this is not new, and yet 'tis *new to me*."

On August 21, 1869, Hudson Taylor responded in his diary:

> How then to have our faith increased? Only by thinking of all that Jesus *is*. and all He is *for us*: His life, His death, His work, He Himself as revealed to us in the Word, to be the subject of our constant thoughts. Not a striving to have faith, or to increase our faith, but a looking off to the Faithful One seems all we need; a resting in the Loved One entirely, for time and for eternity. It does not appear to me as anything new, only formerly misapprehended.

Hudson Taylor was never the same after believing the truth of his oneness with Christ. Shortly after believing this a younger missionary, Mr. Judd, remembers Mr. Taylor's saying to him: "I have not got to *make* myself a branch. The Lord Jesus tells me I *am* a branch I am *part of Him,* and have just to believe it and act upon it."

In a letter dated October 17, 1869 Hudson Taylor wrote to his sister, Amelia:

> "Well, dearie, my mind has been greatly exercised for six or eight months past, feeling the need personally, and for our Mission, of more holiness, life, power in our souls. But personal need stood first and was the greatest. I felt the ingratitude, the danger, the sin of not living nearer to God. I prayed, agonized, fasted, strove, made resolutions, read the Word more diligently, sought more time for retirement and meditation—but all was without effect. Every day, almost every hour, the consciousness of sin oppressed me. I knew that if I could only abide in Christ all would be well, but I *could not.* I began the day with prayer, determined not too take my eye from Him for a moment; but pressure of duties, sometimes very trying, constant interruptions apt to be so wearing, often caused me to forget Him. Then one's nerves get so fretted in this climate that temptations

to irritability, hard thoughts, and sometimes unkind words are all the more difficult to control. Each day brought its register of sin and failure, of lack of power. To will was indeed present with me, but how to perform I found not.

"Then came the question, 'Is there *no* rescue? Must it be thus to the end—constant conflict and, instead of victory, too often defeat?' How, too, could I preach with sincerity that to those who receive Jesus, 'to them gave He power to become the sons of God' (*i.e.* God-like) when it was not so in my own experience? Instead of growing stronger, I seemed to be getting weaker and to have less power against sin; and no wonder, for faith and even hope were getting very low. I hated myself; I hated my sin; and yet I gained no strength against it. I felt I *was* a child of God: His Spirit in my heart would cry, in spite of all, 'Abba, Father': but to rise to my privileges as a child, I was utterly powerless. I thought that holiness, practical holiness, was to be gradually attained by a diligent use of the means of grace. I felt that there was nothing I so much desired in this world, nothing I so much needed. But so far from in any measure attaining it, the more I pursued and strove after it, the more it eluded my grasp; till hope itself almost died out, and I began to think that, perhaps to make heaven the sweeter, God would not give it down here. I do not think I was striving to attain it in my own strength. I knew I was powerless. I told the Lord so, and asked Him to give me help and strength; and sometimes I almost believed He would keep and uphold me. But on looking back in the evening, alas! There was but sin and failure to confess and mourn before God.

"I would not give you the impression that this was the daily experience of all those long, weary months. It was a too frequent state of soul; that toward which I was tending, and which almost ended in despair. And yet never did Christ seem more precious—a Saviour who *could* and *would* save such a sinner! . . . And sometimes there were seasons not only of peace but of joy in the Lord. But they were transitory, and at best there was a sad lack of power. Oh, how good the Lord was in bringing this conflict to an end!

"All the time I felt assured that there was in Christ all I needed, but the practical question was how to get it *out.* He was rich, truly, but I was poor; He strong, but I weak. I knew full well that there was in the root, the stem, abundant fatness; but how to get it into my puny little branch was the question. As gradually the light was dawning on me, I saw that faith was the only pre-requisite, was the hand to lay hold on His fulness and make it my own. *But I had not this faith.* I strove for it, but it would not come; tried to exercise it, but in vain. Seeing more and more the wondrous supply of grace laid up in Jesus, the fulness of our precious Saviour—my helplessness and guilt seemed to increase. Sins committed appeared but as trifles compared with the sin of unbelief which was their cause, which could not or would not take God at His word, but rather made Him a liar! Unbelief was, I felt, *the* damning sin of the world—yet I indulged in it. I prayed for faith, but it came not. What was I to do?

"When my agony of soul was at its height, a sentence in a letter from dear McCarthy was used to remove the scales from my eyes, and the Spirit of God revealed the truth of *our oneness* with *Jesus* as I had never known it before. McCarthy, who had been much exercised by the same sense of failure, but saw the light before I did, wrote (I quote from memory): 'But how to get faith strengthened? Not by striving after faith, but by resting on the Faithful One.'

"As I read I saw it all! 'If we believe *not,* He abideth faithful.' I looked to Jesus and saw (and when I saw, oh, how joy flowed!) that He had said, '*I* will never leave *you.*' 'Ah, there is rest!' I thought. 'I have striven in fain to rest in Him. I'll strive no more. For has *He* not promised to abide with me—never to leave me, never to fail me?' And, dearie, *He never will!*

"But this was not all He showed me, nor one half. As I thought of the Vine and the branches, what light the blessed Spirit poured direct into my soul! How great seemed my mistake in having wished to get the sap, the fulness out of Him. I saw not only that Jesus would never leave me, but that I was a member of His body, of His flesh and of His bones. The vine now I see, is not the root merely, but all—root, stem, branches, twigs, leaves, flowers, fruit: and Jesus is not only that: He is soil and sunshine, air and showers, and ten thousand times more than we have ever dreamed, wished for, or needed. Oh the joy of seeing this truth! I do pray that the eyes of your understanding may be enlightened, that you may know and enjoy the riches freely given us in Christ.

"Oh, my dear sister, it is a wonderful thing to be really one with a risen and exalted Saviour; to be a member of Christ! Think what it involves. Can Christ be rich and I poor? Can your right hand be rich and the left poor? Or your head be well fed while you body starves? Again, think of its bearing on prayer. Could a bank clerk say to a customer, 'It was only your hand wrote that cheque, not you,' or 'I cannot pay this sum to your hand, but only to yourself' No more can your prayers, or mine, be discredited *if offered in the Name of Jesus* (*i.e.* not in our own name, or for the sake of Jesus merely, but on the ground that we are His, His members) so long as we keep within the extent of Christ's credit—a tolerably wide limit! If we ask anything unscriptural or not in accordance with the will of God, Christ Himself could not do that; but, 'If we ask anything according to His will, He heareth us, and . . . we know that we have the petitions that we desire of Him.'

"The sweetest part, if one may speak of one part being sweeter than another, is the *rest* which full identification with Christ brings. I am no longer anxious about anything, as I realise this; for He, I know, is able to carry out *His will,* and His will is mine. It makes no matter where He places me, or how. That is rather for Him to consider than for me; for in the easiest positions He must give me His grace, and in the most difficult His grace is sufficient. It little matters to my servant whether I send him to buy a few cash worth of things, or the most expensive articles. In either case he looks to me for the money, and brings me his purchases. So, if God place me in great perplexity, must He not give me much guidance; in positions of great difficulty, much grace; in circumstances of great pressure and trial, much strength? No fear that His resources will be unequal to the emergency! And His resources are mine, for *He* is mine, and is with me and dwells in me. All this springs from the believer's oneness with Christ. And since Christ has thus dwelt in me heart by faith how happy I have been! I wish I could tell you, instead of writing about it.

"I am no better than before (may I not say, in a sense, I do not wish to be, nor am I striving to be); but I am dead and buried with Christ—aye, and risen too and ascended; and now Christ lives in me, and 'the life that I now live in the flesh, I live by the faith of the Son of God, Who loved me, and gave Himself for me.' I now *believe* I am dead to sin. God reckons me so, and tells me to reckon myself so. He knows best. All my past experience may have shown that it *was* not so; but I dare not say it is not now, when He says it is. I feel and know that old things have passed away. I am as capable of sinning as ever, but Christ is realized as present as never before. He cannot sin; and He can keep me from sinning. I cannot say (I am sorry to have to confess it) that since I have seen this light I have not sinned; but I do feel there was no need to have done so. And further—walking more in the light, my conscience has been more tender; sin has been instantly seen, confessed, pardoned; and peace and joy (with humility) instantly restored: with one exception, when for several hours peace and joy did not return—from want, as I had to learn, of full confession, and from some attempt to justify self.

"And now I must close. I have not said half I would, nor as I would had I more time. May God give you to lay hold on these blessed truths. Do not let us continue to say, in *effect,* 'Who shall ascend into heaven, that is to bring Christ down from above.' In other words, do not let us consider Him as afar off, when God has made us *one with Him,* members of His very body. Nor should we look upon this experience, these truths, as for the few. They are the birthright of every child of God, and no one can dispense with them without dishonour to our Lord. The only power for deliverance from sin or for true service is CHRIST."[1]

---

[1]Quoted material above is from (Dr. & Mrs. Howard Taylor, *Hudson Taylor and the China Inland Mission,* Vol. II, pp. 168-177).

ADDENDUM 3

Youth Discipleship

Goal: to Establish & Maintain friendship w/Christ.

I. Establish
   A. Prerequisites
      1. Salvation
      2. Hunger for Christ—may be generated during process
   B. Preparations
      1. Prepare response sheets for quiet time
      2. Choose accountability method
         a. Using staff or volunteers (best)
         b. Buddy system among teens
            (1) Seniors with sophomores
            (2) Juniors with freshmen
      3. Determine passage
         a. Same passage for all
         b. Choice of staff
         c. Choice of teens
      4. Prepare commitment agreement
      5. Decide if program is mandatory or optional
   C. Proceed
      1. Orient teens with general outline of program
         a. Distinguish
            (1) Soul & spirit
            (2) Walking in the Spirit vs. flesh (Gal. 5)
         b. Explain mechanics
            (1) Importance of reacting to Word (note verbs of Ps. 119 demonstrating writer's reaction to Word)
            (2) How to eat the Word (Jer. 15:16)
               (a) Have a devotional time
               (b) Read respondingly (George Muller)

            i. React to each phrase with confession, thanksgiving, petition, intercession, or worship before going to next phrase
            ii. Record one reaction on response sheet as per example
            iii. Record questions for staff

   2. Challenge to:
      a. Agree to God's authority
      b. Read Word respondingly daily
      c. Sign commitment agreement (return agreement to put in teen's Bible or even frame)
   3. Remind regularly to:
      a. Read slowly—better to camp on a verse for even several days than survey many
      b. Read respondingly
         (1) Not for mental comprehension
         (2) But for spiritual reaction
      c. Memorize a phrase for meditation (Ps. 1)
         (1) A phrase provides an all-day sucker!
         (2) A verse is good for a life time
         (3) A passage provides a menu for a variety of spiritual enjoyments (Ps. 1:2).

II. Maintain
   A. Schedule weekly accountability
   B. Schedule testimony opportunities
   C. Monitor individual progress through staff
   D. Return response sheets to teens to accumulate in a "life" type notebook

ADDENDUM 3B

Commitment Promise

I, ____,
hereby yield myself to God's authority over every area of my life, and I promise to daily read and respond to His Word.

Date ____

ADDENDUM 4

Reading the Bible

Welcome to the Bible—the most important book ever written. It is the greatest book because its content reflects its author, God, and because it changes those who read it (2 Cor. 3:18). Reading the Bible is more beneficial than other books because the Word is the only writing that is inspired by God (2 Tim. 3:16).

There are three methods of reading the Bible. Each has a worthy objective, and in time every believer should employ each of them to some degree. There are numerous variations for each of these methods that can be adapted by each individual.

First, read larger portions to gain familiarity with the themes of the Bible and to get an overview of its teaching. Reading schedules are available at any Christian bookstore, and these can be adapted. The New Testament is the best place to start. It will be helpful to have the benefit of a conservative study Bible for questions that will arise. This type of reading provides balance and an opportunity to enjoy the broad scope of this wonderful Book.

Second, read more slowly than the above method to gain more knowledge of the content. Instead of reading several chapters, read a chapter or less. Take advantage of a commentary on that particular book of the Bible. There are good single volume commentaries you may purchase, and your pastor may be willing to loan you some from his library. It is important that the books you buy or borrow adhere to the traditional, conservative view of interpretation. Unfortunately there is much misleading material written about the Bible by liberals and new evangelicals who have a different agenda.

Third, read the Bible responsively for friendship with God. Although the former two methods need little explanation, this type of reading needs more emphasis because it is the most important of the three methods for every Christian and especially the new and/or young believer. Reading for fellowship with God is so important because God wants that intimacy with you (1 John 1:1-7; John 14:21-23, 15:4-11; Ps. 42:1-5). It is an awesome thought that God has created you to enjoy His company! This is a valuable reason to read this wonderful book.

Now let's think about how to read to see the Lord. Please open your Bible now to Psalm 23:1. Read the first phrase. Stop reading. Talk to God about what He said to you. You may respond to Him with praise for who He is, with thanks for leading you, with confession of the sin of not following Him, or with a prayer for someone you know that needs His leadership right now. Read the second phrase of that verse. Stop reading. As if in conversation with the Author over the phone, answer Him. "I shall not want" means that while following this Shepherd He will provide what I need. You may want to thank Him for His past provisions, for the promise of good things in the future, or for the love that prompted Him to care for you. If you did not open your Bible, please do so now and follow this procedure of responding to each phrase you read in the Psalm.

The Bible is what God wants to say to you. Prayer is what you need to say to God. "Turn the Bible into prayer. Thus, if you were reading the first Psalm, spread the Bible on the chair before you, and kneel, and pray, 'O Lord, give me the blessedness of the man . . . let me not stand in the counsel of the ungodly.' This is the best way of knowing the meaning of the Bible and of learning to pray" (Robert Murray McCheyne).

There are five areas of prayer. **Worship** is praising God for who He is. **Thanksgiving** is recognizing His many blessings. **Confession** is admitting our sins. **Petition** is asking God for what we need. **Intercession** is praying for someone else. To "turn the Bible into prayer" read a phrase or verse, then pray to God in response to what the verse says. For example, if you read something that reminds you of a sin, confess that sin immediately. If the verse makes you think of something you need, ask God for it. If the Holy Spirit draws your attention to another person, spend a short time praying for their needs. If your reading tells you something about God, repeat that back to Him as worship. When you see something God has done for you, give Him thanks. Who God is and what He has done often go together. So worship and thanksgiving are closely related as in Revelation 1:5-6. If you follow this method of reading, you will see the Lord, and your heart can enjoy the One who loves you.

The important thing to remember is that when you read the Bible, God is there in His Word actually communicating with you. Your spirit must he yielded to whatever He says. No one comes into His presence who is not inwardly on his knees. Any other attitude is the result of sinful pride. Although chapters may be read with the mind, God will not be found anywhere. However, He is near the humble (Ps. 51:17). The first step to obeying the Scriptures is to spiritually bow before the God of the Word as you read.

For many years, my devotional time with the Lord was divided into reading the Bible and then praying. I struggled with my mind wandering, with the Bible seeming impersonal, and with being unaware of God's comfort, the brokenness of my spirit, or the Lord's presence. My sinful nature still fights against my desire to commune with God, but this simple plan has helped me greatly.

George Muller in 1897 wrote: "After a few minutes my soul had been led to confession, or thanksgiving, or intercession, or supplication, yet it turned almost immediately to prayer. When thus I have been for a while making confession, or intercession, or supplication, or having given thanks. I go to the next words of the verse, turning all as I go into prayer for myself or others, as the Word may lead to it, but still continually keeping before me that food for my own soul as the object of my meditation."

The most important element for the believer is daily friendship with Christ through the Word.

God has promised that the Holy Spirit will help guide you (John 16:13). As you think about what you have read throughout the day, you will grow like a fruit tree planted by a river (Ps. 1:2-3). With God's help (Heb.13:5-6) you can do this!

ADDENDUM 5

Discipleship Response

Praying the Word with Worship, Thanksgiving, Petition, Confession, Intercession

Date ____________ Verses Read ______________________Responded to ______________________

with: ____

Memorized for the day: ____

Date ____________ Verses Read ______________________Responded to ______________________

with: ____

Memorized for the day: ____

Date ____________ Verses Read ______________________Responded to ______________________

with: ____

Memorized for the day: ____

Date ____________ Verses Read ______________________Responded to ______________________

with: ____

Memorized for the day: ____

Date ____________ Verses Read ______________________Responded to ______________________

with: ____

Memorized for the day: ____

Date ____________ Verses Read ______________________Responded to ______________________

with: ____

Memorized for the day: ____

Date ____________ Verses Read ______________________Responded to ______________________

with: ____

Memorized for the day: ____

ADDENDUM 6—CHAPTER 1

Friendship w/Christ

Addendum 6 provides some teaching helps regarding the main chapters. Before the first meeting, I usually give each person a copy of "Reading the Bible" (Addendum 4) and encourage them to read it and try it! Thereafter I assign a chapter to read. At the beginning of each class I ask for comments and questions from the chapter, which sometimes takes up all the time and actually teaches the class!

The principal idea in Chapter 1 is that Christ is at once the cause and effect of holiness. The purpose of teaching it is to incite a hunger for Christ.

Introduction

Many are telling us what to do; few help us with the how.

- How can I follow Christ today?
- How do I help a co-worker with that?
- How do I lead my family?

Christ is the "what" of the Christian life; friendship w/Christ is the "how."

Only 2 dynamics for which the Christian is responsible:

1. Yielding my spirit to the God of the Word
2. Responding to Jesus first in every circumstance

(If the second is the result of the first, then there is only one. The list of things the Lord does is long!)

The Need

- Daily, personal friendship w/Christ is the most important factor in the Christian's life.
- This is not true of the unbeliever. Why? (Nothing is more important for the unsaved than salvation.)
- Nothing is more rewarding for the believer than to follow Jesus closely, and no bigger failure than being out of fellowship with his Savior.
- There is an alternative to friendship w/Christ.

- The "works of the flesh" (Gal. 5:19-21) are dominant in many believers.
- This dynamic has become their *modus operandi.*
- The HS convicts and we feel terrible, but soothe or ignore our conscience and move on.
- Wrong attitudes become patterns.
- What are some examples of believers following the flesh?

Definition

- The goal here is to get a better handle on this from the bigger picture.
- Friendship w/Christ is the door to communion with the Father (1 John 1:3; Matt. 11:27).
- It is synonymous with abiding in Christ (Jn 15:4), being "filled with the Spirit" (Eph. 5:18), walking in the Spirit (Gal. 5:16), and the believer's "rest" (Heb. 4:9).
- These 5 concepts are similar in Biblical context, cause, and effect.
- God designed us for communion w/Himself.
- Augustine's idea that God has created us for Himself and that our hearts are restless until we find rest in Him is not just for the unsaved.
- All the unsaved of the world are without this peace (Isa. 57:20-21), and we can miss it!
- We have been designed to enjoy communion with God and not with the world.

The Qualification

- Only one—allowing Christ to be our only source.
- The disciple of Christ must be a disciple of no other (Luke 14:26-33).
- What are other potential misguided sources of life?
  - Self-sufficiency
  - Family, Pleasures, Possessions, Church
  - Sinful Tangents
  - Anything That Preempts Christ

Perspective

- Nothing is more important than this.
- We are "complete in Him" alone (Col. 2:10).
- Everything else must find their relevance in Christ alone.
- He is more important than: Prayer, Bible study, obeying God, soul-winning, preaching or listening, family, building the church . . .
- Because all these are the results of fellowship w/Christ.
- We can be full of everything else, yet empty inside.
- Burnout is becoming epidemic . . . why?
- We have repositioned our "first love" (Rev. 2:4).

Distinction

- The difference between seeking God and performing the things of God is the difference between cause and effect.
- Why is it more important to pursue friendship w/Christ than to try to be obedient?

Synopsis of Personal Holiness

- Fellowship w/Christ = first cause of holiness
- HS = agent
- Word = catalyst
- Meditation = method
- Yielding the spirit to the God of the Word = continuing first step
- Everything in these lessons relates to one of these 5 principles.
- (I have found it best to stop here, assign the class or group to read Addendum 1 and 4 for the next meeting, and encourage them to begin to actually follow Muller's suggestion as a daily pattern.)

Summary:

- The Christian life is the result of what God does as we worship Him—not what we do for Him.
- I hope to get the "performance monkey" off your back!

ADDENDUM 6—CHAPTER 2

Relationship of the Word to Friendship

Introduction

- What is the subject of these studies? (Discipleship, befriending Christ, walking w/Christ)
- What is "friendship w/Christ"?
- Where in the believer does this happen? (spirit)
- Today—How does one touch Christ?
- We will cover the role of the Word in this dynamic.
- The method by which we apply the Word is meditation, which is for another day.
- Every believer began his new life in the Word. (1 Pet. 1:23)

I. Functions of the Word—Psalm 119
   A. There are many functions of the Word. These relate to our discussion.
   B. Psalm 119 teaches us the exalted place God has given His Word, the Word's central function to stimulate spirit and life, and man's response to God's communication.
   C. 3 functions of the Word relate to friendship w/Christ:
      1. The Means to seek Him with our "whole heart" (2, 10)
         a. Though God is obvious through creation (Rom. 1), He is hypothetical to the unbeliever and remains anonymous to the believer who does not "seek Him with the whole heart." (= undivided focus)
         b. Jeremiah 29.13
         c. Inseparable from "seeking Him" is "obeying Him" (34, 69).
         d. Is it possible to seek Him without the desire to obey Him?

e. (No—because our spirit must be broken of pride and yielded to approach Him.
f. There are no reservations to a contrite heart.)
g. There is a religious rush among some today on "seeking God."
h. Some churches are identified as "seeker-friendly" churches.
i. Often little, if any, focus is on obedience.
j. In the Bible, believers are identified by obedience rather than seeking.
k. There are attempts to obey the Bible without seeking God.
l. This has been called "performance based Christianity;" i.e. one grows by obeying the Bible.
m. We'll get into this more later, but for now consider that the energy for all the Christian life comes from the Lord, not from us.
n. The Word is the means of seeking God.

2. The Key to an Enlarged Heart (32)
    a. Daily spiritual growth toward maturity in Christ increases our capacity for Him.
    b. There are many perceived worlds.
    c. Every philosophy assumes the nature of things in a certain way.
    d. People create their own view of the world, while God, having revealed in the Word the way it really is, waits for man's acceptance or rejection.
    e. The Word presents the world as it really is.
    f. The more we yield to reality, the more the Lord stretches our capacity.
    g. It is He that enlarges our heart for pursuit, knowledge, and obedience.
    h. God engineers and empowers our maturity according to our association with His Word.
    i. Most believers are discouraged assuming they could never be what God expects.
    j. But what we forget is that it is God who enlarges our heart to run successfully.
    k. The Word enlarges our heart for friendship w/God.

3. Direction for the Godly Heart (36)
    a. The Word is the route we go, the course we follow, our resource for life.
    b. Many substitutes are being sold.
    c. Stores are full of "how to" manuals for the searching soul.
    d. One might get the impression that advice from spiritual gurus, counselors, and handbooks are necessary for a Godward heart.
    e. Many Christians read far more extra curricular material than the Bible itself.
    f. And pulpits are not exempt from "preachers of fortune" selling themselves and their ideas.
    g. Don't forget, only the Bible is inspired by God, and only the Spirit within you can teach you spiritual truth (1 Cor. 2:12-13).
    h. We need to see the Word as "living" (1 Pet. 1:23), and let it become the "joy and rejoicing of (our) heart" (Jer. 15:16).

II. Eating the Word (Ex. 16)
  A. Israel's exodus from Egypt and crossing the Red Sea might be compared to our conversion.
  B. Their wilderness experience is parallel to our sojourn between salvation and heaven.
    1. Our life's path is also through a desert.
        a. We miss many of the consequences of sin as per 15:26.
        b. But this world is no "friend to help us on to God."
        c. "In the world ye shall have tribulation" (John 16:33), and "many are the afflictions of the righteous . . . " (Ps. 34:19).
    2. Israel "murmured."
        a. They sang the "song of Moses" (15:1-19) to praise God for deliverance from Pharaoh's army.
        b. Three days later (15:22) they complained about lack of water (15:24).
        c. The God who controlled the Red Sea could not be trusted to give them drinking water!
        d. We either trust the Lord or our fears; the trusting is the same.
        e. So God tested them with sweet water (15:25), which test they failed, and we find them complaining again in 16:2.

f. They complained because they did not" diligently hearken to the voice of the Lord."
g. How well do we listen to the Lord?
h. God provided "bread from heaven" (4a).
i. Jesus is "the bread of God . . . which cometh down from heaven (John 6:32-35).
j. He is the Word of God (John 1:1), the "only mediator between God and man" (1 Tim. 2:5).
k. They were required to gather it daily (4b).
l. The most important thing in our life is daily friendship w/ Christ in the Word.
m. The Word is the catalyst for the believer's personal holiness.
n. We cannot spiritually prosper for a single day without that infusion of life.
o. To assume that we can make it today by ourselves is to abandon Christ, to take the first step toward shipwreck (1 Tim. 1:6), and to smile at being a "castaway" (1 Cor. 9:27).
p. What are some thoughts we have when we decide to skip a day in the Word?
q. God sustained them with manna for 40 yrs (34).
r. God's provision of grace through the Word is long term.
s. We often forget this simple truth.
t. The life of many believers is like a pendulum swinging regularly between victory in the Word and failure away from it.
u. The most common reason for failure in my life and many others is the lack of consistency.
v. A familiar excuse of many for not pursuing Christ again is their history of failure.
w. True enough when we are the source of our success.
x. But what if God did the sustaining and we only stayed connected to His energy?
y. That we can do long term!
z. The only source of life is God Himself through the Word.

Relation of the Word to Friendship

The goal of this chapter is to raise the stock value of the Word; to emphasize the importance of the Bible to each of us daily.

Introduction

- What is the subject of these lessons?
- What is friendship w/Christ?
- Where in the believer does it happen? (our spirit)
- How does one touch Jesus? (yielding our spirit to the Word)
- Today—the role of the Word in this dynamic; specifically the importance of the Word.
- The method by which we apply the Word (meditation) is for another day.
- Every believer began his new life in the Word (I Pet. 1:23).
- When you were saved, what did the Word do in your spirit?
- Psalm 119 relates many functions.
- This Psalm teaches us the exalted place God has given His Word.
- The Word's central function for believers is to stimulate life in our spirit.

I. 3 functions of the Word that relate to our relationship with Christ

  A. The Means to seek Him with our whole heart (2, 10)

    1. Though God is obvious through creation (Rom. 1), He is hypothetical to the unbeliever and remains anonymous to the believer who does not seek Him with the whole heart (Jer. 29:13).
    2. "whole heart" = undivided focus
    3. It is improbable that we will ever be free from our biases in cultural religion, opinions of theology, and preferences in many areas.

4. But we must learn to give Jesus the priority in all things (Col. 1:18).
5. Coming to the Word to find Him in every truth is a wealth of opportunity to see Him afresh.
6. The Word is the means of seeking and finding God.

B. The Method of enlarging our heart (32)
1. God engineers and empowers our maturity according to our association with His Word.
2. Most believers are discouraged assuming they could never be what God expects.
3. But what we forget is that it is God who enlarges our heart to run successfully.
4. The Word enlarges our heart for friendship w/God.

C. Our Direction (36)
1. It provides the route we go; the course we follow.
2. The Bible can be our resource for life.
3. Many substitutes are being sold.
4. Bible book stores are full of "how to" manuals for the searching soul.
5. One might get the impression that advice of spiritual gurus and handbooks are necessary for a Godward heart.
6. Many Christians read far more extra curricular material than the Bible itself.
7. And pulpits are not exempt from preachers of fortune selling themselves and plagiarized ideas.
8. Don't forget, only the Bible is inspired by God.
9. And only the Spirit within you can teach you spiritual truth (I Cor. 2.12-13).
10. The Word can become "living" (I Pet. 1.23) and the "joy and rejoicing of (our)heart" (Jer. 15.16).

II. Eating the Word (Ex. 16)
A. Israel's exodus from Egypt and crossing the Red Sea might be compared to our conversion.
B. Their wilderness experience is parallel to our sojourn between salvation and heaven.

1. Our life's path is also through a desert (1)
    a. We may miss many of the consequences of sin as per 15.26, but this world is "no friend to help us on to God," and "in the world ye shall have tribulation" (John 16:33).
2. Israel "murmured" (2)
    a. They sang the "song of Moses" (15:1-19) to praise God for deliverance from Pharaoh's army.
    b. 3 days later (15:22) they complained about lack of water (15:24).
    c. The God who controlled the Red Sea could not be trusted to give them drinking water!
    d. So God tested them with sweet water (15:25), which they failed, and we find them complaining again in 16.2.
    e. They complained because they did not "diligently hearken to the voice of the Lord" (15:26).
    f. And that's why we complain.
3. God provided "bread from heaven" (4a)
    a. Jesus is "the bread of God . . . which cometh down from heaven" (John 6:32-35).
    b. He is the Word of God (John 1.1), the "only mediator between God and man" (1 Tim. 2:5).
    c. Jesus is every truth revealing the nature of God (John 14:6).
    d. We meet Him in the Word.
4. They were required to gather it daily (4b)
    a. The most important thing in our life is daily friendship w/ Christ in the Word.
    b. The Word is the catalyst for the believer's personal holiness.
    c. We cannot spiritually prosper for a single day without that life.
    d. To assume that we can make it today by ourselves is to abandon Christ, to take the first step toward shipwreck (1 Tim. 1:6), and to smile at being a "castaway" (1 Cor. 9:27).
5. God sustained them with manna for 40 years (34)
    a. God's provision of grace through the Word is long term.
    b. We often forget this simple truth.
    c. The life of many believers is like a pendulum swinging regularly between victory in the Word and failure away from it.

d. And the religious industry is quick to fill that perceived need with seminars, books, tours, CCM, etc.
e. The only source of life is God Himself through the Word available daily.

The Relation of Friendship to Obedience

Introduction

- Which comes first for the unsaved, obedience or conversion?
- The focus of this lesson is that for the saved, obedience is the result of friendship w/Christ rather than its cause.
- This follows in the wake of the principle that, on the human side, a yielded spirit to the God of the Word is the first cause of holiness, which, by the way, applies to salvation as well as sanctification.
- If obedience were a prerequisite for friendship, it would be assumed that such obedience would come from the individual.
- If fellowship is a prerequisite for obedience, it would follow that such obedience would be sourced in God.
- The relation of friendship to obedience is cause/effect.
- Friendship = cause; Obedience = effect

I. Problem
   A. In almost every other realm . . .
      1. Work goals . . .
      2. Sports . . .
      3. Musical instruments . . .
   B. One might assume . . .
      1. Many unsaved work . . .
      2. Many saved think . . .
   C. What are the consequences . . .
   D. The ability to serve God . . .

II. Distinction
   A. The results of yielding . . .
      1. "Yield-power" is stronger . . .
      2. "Yield-power" = . . .
      3. "Willpower" = . . .

B. The Bible tells us that . . .
    1. Deut. 13.4 . . .
    2. But the responsibility . . .
C. How does John 15.4 suggest . . .
D. Cf. John 12.24-25 . . .
    1. The key to bearing much fruit . . .
    2. Jesus was . . .
    3. Vs. 25 applies Christ's attitude . . .
    4. 2 Cor. 4.11 . . .
E. Will Power
    1. Many substitute . . .
    2. Thayer defines . . .
    3. Scripture does not elevate . . .
    4. "You can do . . .
    5. "Whee there is . . .
    6. "Performance based . . .
F. 3 reasons . . .
    1. Spiritual performance . . .
        a. Nothing in him . . .
        b. He did the opposite . . .
        c. His "delight . . .
    2. Nothing of spiritual permanence . . .
        a. God controls . . .
        b. God incites . . .
        c. We were not saved . . .
        d. Scripture "came not . . .
    3. Jesus did not example . . .
G. Yield Power
    1. Yieldedness is not passive . . .
    2. Obedience not preceded . . .
    3. What is yielded to God . . .
    4. Yieldedness is the . . .

III. Enablement
A. God requires . . .
B. We are responsible to choose . . .

C. But we can't. (His expectations are higher than we think, & our capabilities are lower than we think.)
D. If we recognize the disabling force . . .
E. The weakness of the flesh . . .
F. Rom. 6 = Know, Reckon, Yield
G. Rom. 8.10 summarizes . . .

ADDENDUM 6—CHAPTER 5

Help of the Spirit

The purpose here is to inform the student that there is help available in our quest; that we are not alone in the task. If a child can persuade his parent to help with a chore, it becomes much easier! The Spirit is the helper for personal holiness for every believer.

Unless we are actually enjoying friendship with Christ in the Word daily, these lessons will become academic by default and unhelpful. If one is new to the class and/or church and this idea is new to them, you might provide them some one-on-one.

In the Upper Room Discourse Jesus prepared His disciples for His ascension partly by emphasizing the new role of the Spirit for them. Paul does the same thing in Rom. 8. "More is said in this portion about the Holy Spirit than anywhere else in the NT, except in our Lord's Upper Room Discourse" (Scroggie).

The Christian life cannot work without the Spirit. He is the matchmaker, the facilitator, the enabler.

This is a partial list of how the Spirit helps us in our friendship with Christ from Romans 8.

I. He Rescues us from the sin problem (2)
   A. We cannot walk w/Christ and in sin at the same time (Isa. 59:2, 1 John 1:6-9).
   B. 1 John 1:9 (= "reactionary cleansing)
   C. 1 John 1:7 (= "preventive cleansing)
   D. Some people clean their house after it gets pretty bad, like college students & bachelors! (reactionary)
   E. Others keep their house clean with a daily schedule. (preventive)
   F. The Spirit uses the Word to daily keep us clean.
   G. The "law of the Spirit of life" (8:2) frees us from the power of sin in the flesh (Rom. 6:1-11).

H. Christ's death atoned for the penalty of our sins past, present, & future, so that no one "shall lay any thing to the charge of God's elect. It is God that justifieth" (8:33).
I. Christ's death also conquered our sin nature (6:6).
J. "Since it ('destroyed') is used in this verse of our sinful nature, and in Hebrews 2:14 of the devil, and since both are alive and active, it cannot here mean 'eliminate' or 'eradicate.' It must mean rather that our selfish nature has been defeated, disabled, deprived of power" (John Stott).
K. The Spirit is the force that effects our daily victory over sin.
L. How could that change the attitude of many Christians?

II. He Fulfills the righteous obligation (4)
A. In verse 4 "the righteousness of the law" ("righteous requirement of the law"—Lenski) is that we must "love the Lord thy God" and "thy neighbor as thyself" (Matt. 22:37,39).
B. Romans 13:10—"love is the fulfilling of the law" (ESV).
C. And note that this righteousness is to be "fulfilled in us" (passive voice), not by us.
D. The Spirit is the energy by which we "walk not after the flesh, but after the Spirit."
E. Not only is there sweet communion in fellowship w/Christ, but also almost undetected the Holy Spirit is fulfilling righteousness in us.
F. As He negatively controls the flesh in verse 2, here in verse 4 He positively energizes holiness!
G. We can do neither of these, but we can praise the Lord for His real help!

III. He Defines reality (5)
A. What are some of "the things of the Spirit"? (Jesus, faith, love, forgiveness . . . reality as God sees it)
B. As we "walk . . . after the Spirit", He identifies God's ways, illuminates Christ to us, teaches truth, guides us, and generally keeps us aware of our spiritual environment and needs.
C. He defines this reality to us and keeps us involved with this real world by our connection with Him through the Word daily.
D. We are not "in the flesh" (9) because we are "in the Spirit."

E. But we can be "after the flesh" when we "mind" (think the thoughts of) the world, flesh, or the Devil.
F. We can "mind . . . the things of the Spirit" ("absorbing objects of thought, interest, affection, and purpose"—John Murray).
G. The Spirit helps us by describing God and His interests to us as we "abide in Christ," and we choose to live there.

IV. He Dwells in us (9)
A. Because the Spirit dwells in the believer (9), we are said to be "in the Spirit."
B. We are never without Him or His helps.
C. His presence is unconditionally guaranteed for every believer all the time.
D. His assistance is always available (John 14 :16).
E. "God is our refuge and strength, a very present help in trouble" (Ps. 46:1).
F. Do we feel His indwelling? (no)
G. Then how do we know He does live in us? (the Word & His actions)

V. He Champions for our losing battle (13)
A. Because Christ died to conquer our flesh (6:1-11), and the Spirit has the authority and force to make it happen daily (8:1-11), our responsibility is to allow the Spirit to "mortify the deeds of the body" (8:13).
B. This is our responsibility but requires His power.
C. He is our champion, who stands in for us to "put to death" (8:13—ESV) the attacks through the body of the already conquered flesh (6:6).
D. What are some "works of the flesh"? (Gal. 5, everything done without the Spirit)
E. Without His help none of us could be successful for an hour.

VI. He Leads (14)
A. All the "sons of God" are "lead by the Spirit of God" (8:14), therefore every child of God is "led by the Spirit" (Gal. 5:18).
B. Our Father also controls our way; "He worketh all things after the counsel of His own will" (Eph. 1:11).
C. Believing this gives stability, confidence, and assurance.
D. We cannot have consistent companionship with the Lord if we assume that His presence depends on favorable circumstances.

E. We cannot control our flesh much less the conditions around us.

F. But if He really does lead us through circumstances that He controls, we can rest in Him.

VII. He Adopts (15)

A. Most scholars capitalize the second "Spirit," referencing the Holy Spirit.

B. "Spirit of adoption" is not a name but a function of the Spirit.

C. He brings a new attitude of belonging to individuals in God's family.

D. Why could children in a family of natural birth envy adopted children? (chosen, sometimes paid much for, & sometimes childless couples desire a child more, etc.)

E. We are a "chosen generation" (1 Pet. 2:9), a huge price was paid for each of us, and there is no way to fathom God's desire for us.

F. "The process of legal adoption by which the chosen heir became entitled not only to the reversion of the property but to the civil status, to the burdens as well as the rights of the adopter . . . became, as it were, his other self, one with him. . . . We have but a faint conception of the force with which such an illustration would speak to one familiar with the Roman practice; how it would serve to impress upon him the assurance that the adopted son of God becomes, in a peculiar and intimate sense, one with the heavenly Father" (Merivale, quoted by Vincent).

G. "The Spirit replaces fear with freedom in our relationship to God" (Stott).

VIII. He Assures (16)

A. Satan would love to keep us in doubt of our relationship with our Father.

B. The Spirit bears a strong inward witness to our spirit that we belong to God.

C. In 5:5 the Spirit convinces us of the reality of God's love.

D. Here He convinces us of the reality that we are God's children.

E. "The 'witness of the Spirit' is the producing of the consciousness of being born of God, of belonging to His family, in Christ" (Newell).

F. This witness is not to our minds or emotions, but to our spirit.

G. No need to explain to a child who his parents are.

H. Pointless to ask what love is to an engaged couple.

I. Or to ask why the tear when our flag is raised.

J. There are things that one intuitively knows within his spirit.

IX. He Intercedes (26-27)

  A. The Spirit helps us pray effectively.
  B. He "helps us in our weakness" (ESV).
  C. "Weakness" (singular) may point back to our need to wait patiently for God's purposes (18-25), and/or forward to our ignorance of what to pray for (26b).
  D. "The Spirit lays hand to our infirmity" (Lenski), partially fulfilling His Paraclete job description (John 14:16).
  E. The help He offers in prayer is "as if two men were carrying a log, one at each end" (A. T. Robertson).

ADDENDUM 6—CHAPTER 6

Oneness

Romans 6 = Know something, reckon it so, and yield to the truth

Next time: "reckon," then "yield"

Having itemized the wonderful grace of Jesus in the first 5 chapters, Paul either anticipates a probable reaction or directly confronts a known antagonist to this doctrine of salvation by grace through faith. The objection to be answered in chapter 6 is in v.1. "If salvation is so free, then the more we sin after salvation, the more grace would be required, and God would be exalted."

Paul's answer in capsule form, which he explains in the next 12 verses (v. 2). "It is impossible for anyone to 'live any longer' in sin, who is 'dead to sin.'" vv. 3-10 is Paul's explanation of that statement.

Essentially he says that when Christ died, was buried, and was resurrected, every believer was effectively with Him. In v. 11 he exhorts the believer to accept this truth, and in vv. 12-13 to yield to God.

I. The Fact

A. We were one with Christ in His death, burial, & resurrection. When He died, we died; when he was buried, we were buried; when he was raised, we were raised!

B. It is the author's opinion that there is no water in this chapter, that this is the real thing, of which water baptism is the picture. The picture is not the reality. (v. 3)

C. It's sad that many have seen the picture who have not experienced the real thing!

D. "baptize" = to enter something—those who have partaken of Jesus have entered His death.

E. Cf. Isaiah. 53:10—Either He, by virtue of the resurrection, will one day behold His spiritual posterity; or when He is dying He somehow is aware of those for whom He is dying! That latter interpretation is an awesome thought!

F. As we joined Him in death, so we were buried with Him. (v. 4)

G. "that" = "in order that," suggests a cause/effect relationship . . . we are raised to "newness of life" as He was raised physically. (v. 5)

H. We were "in Christ" even then! "In Christ" is Paul's favorite term to designate the believer's relationship with Christ!

I. Oneness is not conditional, earned, lost, or in any way dependent on us.

J. There will come many times when the believer will doubt what that relationship with Christ really means. During those times, the enemy's darts can be easily sidestepped if we know who we are.

II. The Effect

A. The anticipated (or actual) question deals with continuing in sin (vv. 1 & 2)

B. (v. 6) "old man" = carnal nature, adamic nature, self

C. "destroyed" = "to make inert, idle, inefficient" (Vincent) = render inactive

D. "Since it (destroyed) is used here of our sinful nature, and in Hebrews 2:14 of the Devil, and since both are alive and active, it cannot here mean 'eliminate' . . . It must rather mean that our selfish nature has been defeated, disabled, deprived of power." (John R. Stott)

E. Three steps "To get rid of the self-life" (by F. B. Meyer)

1. The Cross (Rom. 8:3,4)

a. We must believe our oneness with Christ as per Romans 6.

b. "Next to seeing Jesus as my sacrifice nothing has revolutionized my life like seeing the effigy of my sinful self in the sinless, dying Savior."

2. The Holy Spirit (Rom. 8:13, 14)

a. The HS energizes for the defeat of the flesh & exalts Christ.

3. Contemplation of Christ

a. "The one aim of Christianity is to put Christ where man puts self."

b. "The Holy Spirit fixes your thoughts upon Jesus. You do not think about self, but you think much about your dear Lord; and all the time that you are thinking about Him the process of disintegration and dissolution and death of self is going on within your heart."

4. Paul's technique in Ephesians and Colossians is to itemize one's oneness with Christ in the first half of each book and then to encourage us to walk accordingly in the second half.
5. Identity is a huge idea in every culture.
6. Most people are motivated by wanting to be like their heroes, celebrities, or the person in the advertisement.
7. The believer's identity *is* Christ.
8. Quotes regarding our oneness or identity w/Christ:
9. Evan Hopkins: "The trouble of the believer who knows Christ as his justification is not sin as to its guilt, but sin as to its ruling power. In other words, it is not from sin as a load, or an offense, that he seeks to be freed—for he sees that God has completely acquitted him from the charge and penalty of sin—but it is from sin as a master. To know God's way of deliverance from sin as a master he must apprehend the truth contained in the sixth chapter of Romans. There we see what God has done, not with our sins—that question the apostle dealt within the preceding chapters—but with ourselves, the agents and slaves of sin. He has put our old man—our original self-where He put our sins, namely, on the cross with Christ. The believer there sees (Rom. 6) not only that Christ died for him—substitution—but that he died with Christ identification."
10. Andrew Murray: "Like Christ, the believer too has died to sin; he is one with Christ, in the likeness of His death (Rom. 6:5). And as the knowledge that Christ died for sin as our atonement is indispensable to our justification; so the knowledge that Christ and we with Him in the likeness of His death, are dead to sin, is indispensable to our sanctification."
11. L. E. Maxwell: "Believers in Christ were joined to Him at the cross, united to Him in death and resurrection. We died with Christ. He died for us, and we died with Him. This is a great fact, true of all believers."
12. Alexander Hay: "The believer has been united with Christ by his death. In this union with Christ, the flesh, the body of sin—the entire fallen, sin ruined being with its intelligence, will and desires—is

judged and crucified. By faith, the believer reckons (counts) himself 'dead unto sin.'"

13. T. Austin Sparks: "The first phase of our spiritual experience may be a great and overflowing joy, with a marvelous sense of emancipation. In this phase extravagant things are often said as to total deliverance and final victory. Then there may, and often does, come a phase of which inward conflict is the chief feature. It may be very much of a Romans 7 experience. This will lead, under the Lord's hand, to the fuller knowledge of the meaning of identification with Christ, as in Romans 6. Happy the man who has been instructed in this from the beginning."
14. J. Penn-Lewis: "If the difference between 'Christ dying for us,' and 'our dying with Him,' has not been recognized, acknowledged, and applied, it may safely be affirmed that the self is still the dominating factor in the life."
15. Reginald Wallis: "God says in effect, 'My child, as you reckoned on the substitutionary work of the Lord Jesus Christ for your salvation, now go a step farther and reckon on His representative work for your victory day by day.' You believe the Lord Jesus died for your sins because God said so. Now take the next step. Accept by faith the further fact that you died with Him, *i.e.,* that your 'old man was crucified with Him.'"
16. Lewis Sperry Chafer: "Who can fathom the depths of the revelation that the believer is related to Christ on the very plane of that oneness which exists between the Father and Son!
17. "To be 'in Christ' is to be in the sphere of His own infinite person, power, and glory. He surrounds, He protects, He separates from all else, and He indwells the one in Him. He supplies in Himself all that a soul will ever need in time or eternity.
18. "The positions in Christ are never subject to human experience. They produce no sensation by which they may be identified. They are taken by faith, and joyous appreciation may come as a result of believing."
19. John Wesley: "Never think of yourself apart from Christ."

Reckon

Romans 6:11

Chapter 7 deals with the second of the Romans 6 triumvirate. The word, "reckon," conveys something more than a reluctant mental acceptance. The goal for this lesson then is to articulate that distinction, motivating the disciple to pursue reality.

Introduction:

- 3 key words in Rom. 6: Know, Reckon, & Yield.
- Last time "oneness" from John 14:20 was about a larger doctrine of our unity with Christ.
- The Spirit enlightens the believer to "know" that truth.
- Now we look not so much at the meaning of that truth but at how we are to respond to it.
- The subject from 6:1 is victory over the flesh.
- How does "reckon" fit into Paul's teaching about our personal victory
- over our flesh?
- First, faith is not an independent force within us that rises up in time of need.
- Faith rides on an object; it must be attached to a truth.
- It is not something we look for within us, but our response to an objective proposition.
- The unbeliever has faith that hell is a myth.
- We believe that God is, and that everything He says is true.
- Faith happens when properly attached to a truth.
- Second, knowing the stated facts of our spiritual conflict is not sufficient to win the battle.
- We must respond to those facts as per "reckon" and "yield."

I. Reckon
   A. What does it mean?
   B. This word implies more than being aware of something, and includes a response to that something.
   C. It is "an expression of belief, and of an attitude in view of that belief" (William R. Newell).
   D. Thayer says it means "to account and treat accordingly."
   E. So, there is a preliminary mental acceptance of a fact, and then a response to it.
   F. John Murray wrote, "we are to reckon with and appreciate the facts, which [we] already obtain by virtue of union with Christ."
   G. Being aware of our oneness with Christ, we are now encouraged to take hold of it with an attitude!
   H. Most of us know more than we have reckoned.
   I. To "reckon" is the expected progression of faith.
   J. It is the beginning of obedience of which James spoke—not faith alone, but faith evidenced (Jas. 2:18).

II. Reckon yourselves dead to sin
   A. How are we "dead to sin?"
   B. The stated problem deals with "continuing in sin" (v. 1).
   C. Those who are "dead to sin" do not live any longer in it (v. 2).
   D. Dead people don't walk around except on TV!
   E. Saved people do not "live in sin."
   F. "No one who keeps on sinning has either seen him or known him" (1 John 3:6—ESV).
   G. The "body of sin" (v. 6) is the power-house of sin in the unsaved described in vv. 9 and 14 as "dominion" that has been conquered for the believer by Christ on the cross.
   H. Many believers are not persuaded that their carnal nature has been brought under control by Christ on the cross.
   I. Their few attempts to step up to the plate spiritually have not been lasting.
   J. Their disappointments have colored their expectations and their view of themselves.
   K. They do not believe that v. 6 applies to them.
   L. The primary idea of "dead" is separation, not cessation.

M. The physically dead are separated from the living.
N. They have not ceased to exist.
O. We are "dead to sin"; because, when the authority of our sin nature was conquered, it was separated from its power to control.
P. "The apostle does not say that sin is dead to us, but that we in Christ are dead to it" (W. H. Griffith Thomas).
Q. "Your relationship to sin is exactly the same as Christ's!" (Newell)

III. Reckon yourselves alive to God
  A. "alive" = spiritual life = that spiritual flow of the Spirit moving through my spirit.
  B. "unto God"—states to or for whom something is done (dative). The object of this life is to glorify God; not us!
  C. "through Jesus Christ"—"in" is a better translation.
    1. "In Christ" is Paul's favorite description of the believer, especially in the books of Ephesians and Colossians.
    2. We are "in Christ."
    3. We have crawled up into His heart and into His kingdom.
    4. In such a position our sinful nature is not in control any more.
    5. Here the superior energy dominates.
    6. If you believe that is a fact, will you respond with worship and obedience?

Conclusion:

- Ask yourself, "Do I have a proactive attitude toward Christ and against my sin?" (one question; not two)
- "Does my knowledge of truth direct my lifestyle?"
- The Church is laden with believers who know the facts but are not spiritually motivated.
- They don't have a positive attitude.
- They have no fire in the soul.
- They are acceptable in their religious environment but have no "hunger and thirst after righteousness."
- From this pool come those who are satisfied with mediocrity, who have no spiritual impact on their neighbors, who are easy victims

of Satan's schemes, and who grow old and often bitter toward God and His Church.

- And worse, we can do nothing to defeat our enemy or revive ourselves.
- The only workable advice is to "look to Jesus"—learn to "gaze" on Him.
- When we contemplate Christ, to quote Meyer again, "all the time that you are thinking about Him, the process of disintegration and dissolution and death of self is going on within your heart."
- Other Quotes
  - "Practical deliverance is not found by fighting with the old master, sin in the flesh, but by the daily recognition of the truth.
  - "Reckon . . . means literally 'count as true'" (Harry Ironside).
  - "Sanctification does not progress because of self determination or will-power; it progresses as Christ and the benefits of His sacrifice are appropriated by faith.
  - "Reckon . . . emphasizes the vital appropriation of what is believed. It is one thing to believe something to be generally true; it is another thing to regard it as personally true" (Michael Barrett).
  - "The Christian's breaking with sin is undoubtedly gradual in its realization, but absolute and conclusive in its principle" (Godet).
  - "We are not to pretend that our old nature has died, when we know perfectly well it has not. Instead we are to realize and remember that our former self did die with Christ, thus putting an end to its career.
  - "We are to recall, to ponder, to grasp, to register these truths until they are so integral to our mindset that a return to the old life is unthinkable. Christians should no more contemplate a return to unregenerate living than adults to their childhood, married people to their singleness, or discharged prisoners to their prison cell" (John Stott).

Yield

The object of this chapter is to define yieldedness of spirit, distinguish it from its effects in the soul, and articulate what it looks like for the believer. The challenge for the teacher is to convey that an agreement in the mind, a feeling in the emotions, or a decision in the will is not this.

Introduction

- Friendship w/Jesus happens in the spirit before that life effects our life.
- What are some Godly things we can do without God? (attend church, give, help others, be friendly, etc.)
- Since a yielded spirit to the God of the Word is the first cause of holiness (from the human perspective), how holy are we, when our religion is motivated by the flesh?
- Distinguish self-righteousness and the righteousness of faith in salvation and sanctification as in Romans 8:2-4.

Definition

- You might try to mimic an OT priest lifting up some offering or raising a male child in both hands up to God.
- We yield every part of us by giving it up to the Lord.
- Our life is to be spent giving over everything to Him. Anything less is rebellion.
- Jesus Did!
- Psalm 22:8 is fulfilled in Matthew 27:43 by the reviling crowd around the cross.
- Apparently Jesus referenced the Father so many times in their presence that Jesus' trust in the Father began to stick in their craw!
- We can well follow the Lamb here.
- He trusted the Father for speech (John 8:26), actions (v. 29), motivation (v. 49), and identity (v. 50).
- Hard to Do?

- Expect some push back on the idea that it is as easy to yield to the Lord as it is to the flesh. Emphasize that the essence of both is the same.
- Walking on either side of a fence is easy. Trying to walk on both sides is hard!
- Self-righteousness is hard, but it's easy for us when the energy of the Spirit controls us.

Order of Yieldedness

- Some relate "yield yourselves" to salvation and "your members" to everything involving sanctification.
- The important thing here is that our "members" are the hundreds of parts of us making up each day! There is no way each item of every day can get individual attention.
- We are creatures of habit.
- The only hope is to stay connected to Jesus in the Word by meditation.
- This sets and maintains an constant attitude of submission to the Lordship of Christ.
- It becomes a subconscious "well of water springing up" (John 4:14) all the time.

On Being Slaves

- The assumption that we are a third power for serving God is hard to demote but absolutely necessary.
- The issue is humility vs. pride.

ADDENDUM 6—CHAPTER 9

Meditation

If I had but one message I could preach to hungry believers, this is it! This is where "the rubber hits the road." If I could encourage one habit in a believer it would be meditation. This will become the object of accountability for those you will disciple. Your students should by now be practicing meditation and probably will have some excuses. In chapter 13 there is a list of excuses I have heard and used. You might familiarize yourself with them.

Method

- Understanding the Biblical method of meditation is not hard. It's the challenge of consistency.
- More people in our culture understand yoga today than ever before.
- Don't confuse pagan teachings on awareness and this Bible method of becoming aware of God.

Better Way

- You can preach this!
- In the final analysis, the success of the believer is determined by his/her attitude toward the God in the Word.
- How Long?
- This is where some will check out. They can't understand how to focus on the Lord and get everything else done.
- This is just another opportunity to multitask.
- The key is to invest quality time seeing Jesus in the Word spiritually and mentally.
- In time the spiritual will become a subconscious attitude that flavors the mental even when it is totally focused.
- You might remind them that no believer walks in the Spirit all the time, at least I don't know of anyone who does, though several make that claim! I think it was Scofield who said, "The up and down experience is not the Christian experience, but it is every Christian's experience."
- Are we Really Slaves?
- Most adults are just as selfish as children. We just cover it better.

ADDENDUM 7

Chapter Questions

Chapter 1

1. What is the most important need in the Christian's life?
2. What is the most important need in the unbeliever's life?
3. What are some "works of the flesh" other than listed in Gal. 5?
4. Is Christ the only way to know the Father?
5. What other sources can a believer have other than Jesus?
6. How can Christians assume Christ, yet not follow Him?
7. What are the three methods of reading the Bible?
8. Which method is most important to the disciple?
9. How does one integrate reading the Bible and praying?
10. What are the five areas of prayer?

Chapter 2

1. Describe a yielded spirit.
2. Is it possible to follow Christ and not be submitted to Him?
3. Describe a religious person whose spirit is not yielded.
4. What is our soul?
5. Why must we yield our spirit before following Jesus with our mind, will, and emotions?
6. Is following Christ what we do or what the Spirit does through us?
7. Have you tried to do something for Christ and failed?
8. In Romans 6:18 how many powers are there?
9. Are there any neutrals in this power structure?
10. How can I become a servant of the Lord?

Chapter 3

1. How is the Bible related to friendship with Jesus?
2. Why do some new believers lose the joy of their salvation?
3. Am I addicted to my sin nature?
4. Who conquered my sin nature and when?
5. Randomly choose a Psalm 119 verse and find why the Word is important?
6. How do we get close to the Lord today?

7. How does the Word reflect the nature of the Lord?
8. How does God change us to be successful?
9. Why is the Word more important than sermons, Christian music, and Christian leaders?
10. How is the manna in the wilderness like the Word?

Chapter 4

1. Does the energy source to obey come from us or from the Spirit?
2. What is the difference between believer's and the unbeliever's energy source to succeed?
3. Distinguish "willpower" from "yield-power."
4. "The key to bearing 'much fruit' is ______________________________."
5. Why are we not exempt from the responsibility to obey God even though we don't have the ability?
6. What is "performance-based" sanctification?
7. Why does willpower fail us?
8. Why is Galatians 5:16 the key to victory over our flesh?
9. Why do many believers quit trying to follow Christ?
10. Why is trying to obey without the enabling Spirit self-righteousness?

Chapter 5

1. Where did we get our "Adamic nature"?
2. Who conquered my sinful nature and when?
3. Who is our enabler for spiritual success?
4. Distinguish "preventive cleansing" from "reactionary cleansing."
5. In Romans 8:4 is the "righteousness of the law" fulfilled "by" us or "in" us?
6. How do we set our minds on "the things of the Spirit"?
7. What happens when we are not "spiritually minded" (KJV)?
8. How do we "put to death" the deeds of the flesh?
9. Does the Lord control the path we walk?
10. With what does the Spirit assure us that we are children of God.

Chapter 6

1. What does God see when He sees us?
2. In your own way describe "oneness."
3. What is the key NT passage on sanctification?
4. How were we one with Christ in Rom. 6:1-8?
5. What does it mean to be "in Christ"?

6. Faith is strengthened by "______________________________" (Hudson Taylor).
7. "We may make __________________ of our partnership" with God (George Muller).
8. F. B. Meyer suggests that we:
9. "_______________ my self-life to the cross"
10. "_______________ on the Spirit"
11. "_______________ Christ"

Chapter 7

1. What are the three primary words in Romans 6?
2. Why do some leave the Lord when they leave home?
3. Why do some seniors get tired of serving the Lord?
4. What is the difference between knowing something with the mind and reckoning it with the spirit?
5. Why do we know more than we obey?
6. How do I "appraise myself dead to sin"?
7. How do I "appraise myself alive to Christ"?
8. Do I "hunger after righteousness"?
9. What does it mean to "look unto Jesus"?
10. From John Stott's last quote distinguish between a mental belief and a spiritual belief.

Chapter 8

1. What is man's supreme sin?
2. When do I do that?
3. What is the antidote?
4. How do we "yield" to God?
5. What is the opposite of independence of God?
6. Is it hard to obey the Lord when your spirit is yielded to His Word?
7. Is there any neutral ground between yielding to God and yielding to Satan?
8. Why does a lifestyle of obedience or sin distinguish the saved from the unsaved? (cf. 1 John 3:9)
9. When has willpower failed you?
10. Why do you think God honors a yielded spirit?

Chapter 9

1. What is the difference between Eastern meditation and Biblical meditation?

2. What is common in Biblical meditation and listening to music constantly with ear buds?
3. According to Joshua 1:8 what is necessary for obedience?
4. Do I "delight" in seeing the Lord in the Word as much as watching my favorite TV program?
5. How many times a day do I remember the Lord?
6. How does meditation help in remembering?
7. Is Christ my way or an additive for my own way?
8. What can help me meditate better?
9. What is my greatest satisfaction now, which I hope to demote?
10. What do I do when I fail at this?